The People Between

by

Jacob Minasian

Finishing Line Press
Georgetown, Kentucky

The People Between

*For my wife
and for my daughter*

Copyright © 2025 by Jacob Minasian
ISBN 979-8-89990-073-0 First Edition
All rights reserved under International and Pan-American Copyright Conventions. No part of this book may be reproduced in any manner whatsoever without written permission from the publisher, except in the case of brief quotations embodied in critical articles and reviews.

ACKNOWLEDGMENTS

Thank you to my wife and to my mother, always my first readers.

Publisher: Leah Huete de Maines
Editor: Christen Kincaid
Cover Art: Jacob Minasian
Author Photo: Helena Minasian
Cover Design: Elizabeth Maines McCleavy

Order online: www.finishinglinepress.com
              also available on amazon.com

Author inquiries and mail orders:
Finishing Line Press
PO Box 1626
Georgetown, Kentucky 40324
USA

Contents

Prologue

Freddie 1

Part One

Bartley 11

Wisecracker 17

Christopher 21

Bartley and Marlene 28

Marlene and Christopher 31

Bartley 34

Joseph 38

The Sown 44

Part Two

Bartley 57

The Keepers 63

The Reaped 69

In the near future, over 78% of Earth is compromised by some category of natural disaster at all times. The Automated Radio Weather System is the only warning the surviving humans have, the only way they know which locations will be safe, and the routes to get to them. And with California and the majority of the east coast underwater due to rising sea levels, there are less places to go...

Prologue

Freddie

Freddie "Jammer" Jamison coasted into the barren kidney-shaped parking lot in his filthy silver Toyota Prius, just beyond the banks that sloped down to the recently storm-fattened, now already retreating waterline of the Ohio River, his hands shaky on the plump steering wheel, his right foot timing a quick acceleration over one of the lot's outer dividers before he jerked the steering left, the front wheels turning almost parallel against the short cement perimeter. He pulled the keys from the ignition and stepped out into Cincinnati.

Freddie was precise in his arrival, as he liked to be—the Automated Radio Weather System being the new design of his existence. The monstrous storm had exited the area less than a day earlier, and the air was thick with small flying bugs—gnats or midges, he guessed—clouds and endless ribbons of them stirred by the heavy rain. He pulled up the handkerchief from around his neck to cover his mouth, lowered the UV sport sunglasses from the top of his head to cover his eyes, and stepped around to the car's trunk to retrieve his mountaineering backpack, the straps of which he tightened over each shoulder, and his orange-black Orioles baseball cap, which he secured over his sweaty shoulder-length mop of reddish-brown hair, kneading the bend in the brim with both hands.

Walking inland across the parking lot, his Adidas scraping softly on the asphalt cracked by earth and weeds, Freddie looked up at the punishing sun, then over his shoulder at the grading drop to the murky edge of the sun-beat river. The C.W. Bailey Bridge, the only bridge left standing between Kentucky and Ohio despite its smaller size, stretched across the water like a bloodily humbled victor, its cement and steel holding against unfavorable odds. Rusted machinery from a long-closed quarry protruded out into Freddie's sightline, piercing the desolate landscape, a dissolving monument to its now defunct purpose.

The humidity hung on Freddie like an uncomfortable hug.

"You know," he said, stepping over the chunks of an obliterated concrete blockade. "You know when you're just trying to get to the next clear zone, and a group of pirates flanks your vehicle, and 'asks' for your gas?" He waited, his hands lowering from his finger-hooks around the word "asks." Then, "Yeah, me too." He paused. "Well, I told this particular group of pirates —there were three of them in one of those, you know, really groovy Humfire SUVs, the kind that helped melt the planet—anyway, I told them 'So, are you saying you want me to *pass gas*?' And I'm telling you, they laughed. I shit you not, they were full-on belly laughing. That's right. Yeah." He gave a half-hearted arm-twirl to the imaginary crowd, paused again. "And then they shot me in the leg and left me for dead—ba dum bum chhh." He kicked a small mound of rubble as he mimicked the sound of a punchline rimshot.

He wrangled his keys out of the left pocket of his cargo shorts, almost subconsciously, rotated and parsed the ringed collective of laser-shaped metal until he had the comedian key-charm between his left thumb and forefinger. He squeezed, and a post-joke rimshot sounded from the tiny speaker. His thumb moved over the words "Guaranteed Funny!" stamped into the plastic.

"Ha ha ha," he said, crossed a narrow street, and headed toward the towering concrete remains of Paycor Stadium, which once housed the gladiatorial helmet-hammering of football franchises, until increasing medical findings forced rules that dried up the fan-base, cut the number of teams, and caused the massively profitable league to hemorrhage airtime and ticket sales until it was boiled down to its eight most profitable teams. The other franchises, pushing the new-age rules even further, attempted to form their own league, the Electro-Touch Football League, which inevitably gave way to the higher audience numbers for concerts and entertainment events playing in their stadiums.

Freddie crossed through the area where the ticket gates and vendor booths had been torn from their placements, walked toward the sloping entrance to the lower access tunnels around the stadium. He paused, stepped into the stadium's shade, thumbing his keychain. He raised his other hand to his chin, fingers finding way through his auburn beard to scratch skin.

"Who said that the Maine coastline wasn't absolutely spectacular in the fall?" he said, pausing. "Well, my brother and his family, who all drowned in the famous Atlantic Collapse! I mean, who even needs a tsunami, right guys?" He pointed into the stadium cement at an imaginary audience. "Yeah, there it is, you in the third row, you get me!" He squeezed a comedic rimshot from the keychain trinket's speaker. "That fall into the ocean is a bitch."

As he walked into the mouth of the tunnel, his right hand lowered to the handle of the .45 caliber Colt Peacemaker in its 1800s-style leather belt holster, the belt buckled loosely so the holster dipped slightly below his waistline. He palmed the polished oak grip, his thumb on the ridges of the metal hammer. His left hand pocketed the keychain, raised his sunglasses to rest over the brim of his baseball cap. His eyes scanned the tunnel's inner bowels, intervallic supporting cement slabs to his right, indented wall widening the tunnel to his left. Trash trembled in the soft wind the tunnel picked up and carried in from the outside. The coolness was a relief, even more than Freddie had hoped. He could shelter here. But that made him worry.

As he walked, Freddie whispered, "Why did the chicken cross the post-apocalyptic road?" His vision trimmed the far corners of the shade. "Wait, there's a chicken? Let's deep-fry that son of a bitch!" He heard the dull echo of a heavy shoe sliding across cement. "Ba dum chhh."

He unholstered his revolver. Wiggled his wrist. The barrel of the gun wagged.

As soon as he heard the male voice, before he could ascertain content or meaning, he raised his pistol and fired in its direction.

"Woah! Woah! Wait!" the voice, panicked, cried as Freddie's wildly low shot ricocheted off the floor and ate itself into some concrete portion of the shadows.

Freddie fired again, knowing he was either establishing power in this interaction or ending it altogether. The gun's recoil bit into his hand and wrist. He heard nothing from the second bullet, though more pleas from the shadows. He resettled himself and aimed into the darkness.

"Please! *Please!*" the voice said.

After a few heartbeats, a man stepped forward into the shallow light, knees bent, head ducked, hands held shoulder height, palms facing Freddie.

As the man lifted his face—angular jaw, hazel eyes, a deeply retreating hairline—Freddie recognized him immediately. He was in his late forties, wearing a dirt and sweat scored white shirt and dark blue jeans over a muscular medium-height frame.

"Oh, shit, it's you! It's you, right? Uh, uh, Aaron!" Freddie kept the gun barrel level with the man's chest.

He had never met a celebrity before.

The man trembled. "Alan," he said.

"That's right, that's right. Aaron was the other one, right? Aw, man, I can't believe it's you!"

Alan tilted his head in a small diagonal nod. Sweat bristled his forehead, ran from his sideburns.

Freddie looked at his handgun, back to Alan's eyes. "You're cool, right? I mean, I remember reading about you. Stand-up guy, right?"

Alan blinked, flexed his eyebrows. "Yeah. Yeah, of course. Sure."

"So, I can put this away, right?" Freddie nodded at the revolver. "I didn't mean to scare you. I just, I mean, you know."

"Yeah. Yeah, I'm cool. In fact, I even got some food. Be more than happy to share a little if you want. We can just sit on down and eat and talk. Sound good?"

Freddie holstered his pistol. His pack was heavy against his shoulders with his large stock of canned beans. He was sick of beans.

"Sounds good," he said, and smiled. He rubbed his hands together. "So what are we having?"

Alan leaned toward the darkness. "Come on. I have plenty of beans."

#

As Freddie looked down into the can of cold lima beans, eyes having adjusted to the tunnel's shadows, the refried beans and baked beans sitting in his pack didn't seem as unappetizing as before. He oared the white beans with his plastic spoon, scooped some to his mouth, glancing over at Alan, who sat on the cement floor just a few feet from him, stabbing a spoon into his own open can, leaning against the wall of the tunnel.

"So then I said," Freddie said, still chewing, "'So you're telling me to *pass gas*?'" He studied Alan's face, who smiled obligingly. "Right? Funny?"

"Yeah," Alan said. "That's funny."

Satisfied, Freddie took another bite. After swallowing, "So what's it like?"

"What?" Alan turned his spoon over in his can.

"You know, being the first—and only, I guess, right?—cloned human, ever. What's that like?"

Alan glanced at the ground in Freddie's direction. "It's complicated."

"Aw, man. I bet. I remember the search they did, all the litigation, the votes. Should we clone the best athlete, the most genius scientist, the president? And then they go with you, because why?"

"I'm average."

"Not just average. The most average son-of-a-bitch in the country—according to them, at least. Middle age, middle class, small business owner."

"You remember a lot."

"Shit, I was writing jokes about it! No offense, I mean."

"Should have never thrown my hat in the ring. Filled out that online form on a whim...and a not so small nudge from my wife."

"Yeah? I guess she loved you so much she wanted two of you." Freddie paused. "Fucked up what they did to your clone though."

Alan didn't answer.

"Even *I* couldn't have written a joke about that," Freddie said.

Alan's forehead flinched. He stirred his beans. "They murdered him. Showed up at his house in plain daylight. Like villagers with torches coming after Frankenstein's monster. Called him an abomination. Unholy. And burnt him alive in his own home."

Freddie watched Alan's face. "Shit. No wonder they shut down the program after that."

"Yeah. Well, that's not the most fucked up part." Alan leaned toward Freddie. "No one knows this—no one still alive at least—but later I learned that I was... I am the clone."

Freddie's eyes swelled. "I knew the original guy's name was Aaron!"

"They deliberately misinformed us about which one we each were, for their fucking 'clinical purposes.' To see how convincing and convinced we were. So I was having a beach day with his family while he burned."

Freddie put a hand to his forehead, his jaw hanging open. "Shit!"

"Yeah," Alan said. He paused. Freddie stared at him. After a few more seconds, Alan continued, "I was outraged when I found out. I mean, *outraged*. Almost spilled it to every news outlet filling up my voicemail. But their little guise—their little clinical trick—saved my life. A life they created to begin with. I know it's fucked up, but some small piece of me was grateful."

"Damn," Freddie said. "Yeah, I get that."

#

"You ready, brother?" It had been ten days since Freddie had driven into Cincinnati, had run into Alan. Now it was time to leave and head south.

"Yeah, I think so." Alan looked around the tunnel, hooked his thumbs into the straps of his pack. "Ready when you are."

They had decided two days earlier to travel together.

Freddie tossed a worn football lightly from one of his hands to the other. While rummaging through the stadium to augment their supplies, they had found a spilled rack of footballs in the corner of an equipment room, and had taken turns throughout the empty days' light running routes out on the hard dried dirt of the stadium's field, showboating like wide receivers while the other person played star quarterback and threw slants, button hooks, and Hail Mary's.

"Let's go then," Freddie said. "My car first, then we'll swing by yours for the gas."

"Copy that," Alan said.

After their first interaction, they had bunkered deeper into tunnel, and now walked the long arcing left turn back to the tunnel's entrance, exiting and stepping out of the shade into the warming light. They passed through the stadium's entry area and stepped out onto the sidewalk bordering the narrow street Freddie had crossed ten days before, both of them wearing sunglasses, both of them moving with a newfound confidence now that they were no longer traveling alone.

A woman's voice screamed, "*Hey! Don't fucking move!*"

Both their heads turned to the right, saw a small group of people—three women and two men, all heavily armed—about sixty yards up the street in the direction of downtown Cincinnati, the imperative coming from a woman carrying a clip-fed shotgun.

"Oh," Freddie said to Alan, strained sarcasm, "now what do you suppose she wants?"

The woman, a monstrous anger dissociated from reality coiling in her features, raised the shotgun and fired, inconsequential due to the distance and the weapon's range.

"Run," Alan said, his hand gripping his pack's straps over each shoulder. "Freddie, *run!*" And he turned in the direction of the river and ran.

Freddie ran with him.

"Go get 'em, Stace! Get 'em, Hank!" One of the men yelled, loud, as if it was also for Freddie and Alan. "The newlyweds, getting their first kills!"

Sprinting next to Alan, his revolver jostling against his thigh, Freddie said, "Did he just fucking say, '*newlyweds?*'"

Alan didn't look back. "Shoot them," he said. "*Shoot them!*"

"You kidding?" Freddie shouted back. "I'm a comedian, not a gunslinger. You saw. I can't shoot worth shit! Only thing safe is what I'm aiming at!"

The Ohio River's dip in the landscape was now in sight.

Freddie looked over his shoulder. The woman with the shotgun and one of the men, who also wielded a shotgun, were both in pursuit.

An old joke flooded Freddie's mind, the one about not outrunning the bear, just the guy next to you.

He and Alan were both at a full sprint, Alan a step ahead. Freddie glanced at the side of Alan's face.

As he ran, Freddie pulled his revolver from its holster, aimed it at Alan's left knee, and pulled the trigger. The gun bucked—the bullet missed the knee, but hit Alan's right calf.

"*Ah!*" Alan yowled in pain and surprise, his leg giving way, his face and torso falling from Freddie's periphery into the sound of his body hitting fragmented earth.

Another shotgun blast sounded. Freddie continued to run, past his Toyota Prius, toward the river, down the unforgiving slope, feeling the shocks of his heels bouncing against dirt and stone and broken cement hammer up through his legs, until he reached the murky waterline of the river, and dove in.

He suppressed his breath against his accelerated pulse and waited in the current below the surface, rising only for a few short swills of oxygen.

About three football fields' length down the river, Freddie emerged, dripping brown water, pulling at the straps of his backpack, coughing and gagging from the stench. His hat and sunglasses lost in the water, he wrung out his hair and began walking the bleak bank of the river, thinking how he might get back to his car, sunlight slowly drying him. There was little time before the acid rain would sweep into the expiring clear zone with an acidity level far higher than anyone thought possible in the old world.

As he walked, he reached into his pocket, brought out his keychain, his fingers instinctively finding the comedian charm, the guaranteed rimshot, water leaking out of it, and he squeezed, though it was broken.

No rimshot. No imaginary laughs.

Part One

Bartley

The storms carried the stripped bones of the dead and laid them where they chose.

A femur showed alone and distant from its human housing, clean white between spatters of soil, as polished as driftwood from a foreign shore, lying slant against the partially uprooted leg of a massive lodgepole pine, deep within the boundaries of what was once called Yellowstone National Park.

Bartley sat leaning against a fallen trunk of the same breed of tree, staring at the upper-leg bone, knowing it was human, knowing it must have been dropped there shortly before he and his group had arrived. Throughout his career as a chef in the old world fading from memory faster with each new day, he had pulled the bones from almost every edible earthly creature, including much of Yellowstone's local fauna—buffalo, elk, rabbit, even squirrel—none of which he or his group had seen any traces of on their way into the clear zone.

His stomach burned cold from the sight of the femur.

He refocused his attention back to what he could see of the 38 people wandering warmly among the freshly propped town of generously spaced tents, some still arranging the canvas and coolers and bedding they all had unpacked from their fleet of vehicles—four coups, six SUVs, and five large utility vans. The people were worn from travel and their individual histories, clothes filthy and frayed, much of their skin littered with scars, but they still shimmered with a collective optimism.

And their numbers grew with every new clear zone.

Nine years now into this new world, with the human population pushed to numbers nearing extinction, the earth had begun to heal—the natural disasters still prevalent but beginning to relent, the clear zones tracked by the ARWS more abundant and longer lasting, some even holding for months. This easement had allowed many of the frightened and more peaceful survivors to find one another, to group together and travel as small communities, increasing their odds against the elements, and against the brutal belly of humanity that desired violence.

Bartley nodded to himself, brought a cigarette to his lips from the pack in his breast pocket, lit it with his Zippo. His eyes moved to the landscape beyond the encampment, to the hills and distant mountains covered in the shards of burned forest and large swaths of bare land carved by tornados, trees uprooted and flattened or carried away. There were only small scattered patches of trees still standing. The group had built their camp near one of those patches, a bare flat clearing of Yellowstone's volcanic plateau stretching out to the west, steam rising from the pools in its surface in the late afternoon sunlight. Three times now they had seen the distant eruption of a large geyser in the distance, what Bartley assumed was the one named "Old Faithful," a gigantic column of water rising from the earth like an upward turned firehose, blooming into a wide cloud of spray and steam at the top.

As Bartley's eyes lowered back to the camp, he caught sight of a group member smaller than the rest, a blur of blonde hair bounding through the array of tents and turning up the gentle slope to where Bartley sat against the fallen tree. Bartley quickly pinched the cherry off of his cigarette and ground it with his boot. The four-year-old girl in a faded pink dress and yellow shoes lifted an old glass jam jar as she ran.

"Bartley, Bartley, look! Spotsy! She's eating!" the girl said, and held the jar toward Bartley.

Bartley smiled, placed a hand briefly on the top of her head, took the jar from her and studied the few green leaves and solitary ladybug within the glass. There were small tears in the leaves.

"Oh yeah," he said. "She's looking like she's fattening up. Much healthier." He handed the jar back to her. "You know, usually it's good luck for a person to find a ladybug. But I think it's the other way around here. I think it was good luck for Spotsy to've found you."

Her small face brightened with pride. "Thanks, Bartley." She stared into the jar, held it close to her eyes. "I love her."

"She loves you too, Charlotte. I can tell."

Charlotte laughed.

"Char!" Charlotte's mother, Marlene, called out from the edge of the camp. She spotted her daughter. "Char, come on. It's dinnertime for you, let's go."

"Okay, mom! Bye, Bartley."

"Bye, Charlotte. Have a good dinner." He looked up at Marlene, who smiled at him as Charlotte bounced back down to the camp. Marlene turned and she and Charlotte disappeared among the tents.

Bartley relit his cigarette.

"Bartley," a voice came from behind him, further up the slope. Bartley exhaled smoke, turned his head, chin parallel to his shoulder. Joseph, one of the group's foragers, stepped next to him and crouched down. "Hey, we found these." He held up a single dark brown mushroom with a long pocked cap between his thumb and forefinger. "There's a bunch of them scattered up there near some of the trees. What do you think? They safe?"

Bartley's features seemed to squeeze together in his examination. "Black morels. Oh yeah. Good find. They'll make a great soup. They have a kind of nutty flavor. I'll cook it myself."

"Shit yeah. Now that's what I wanted to hear; damn sure looking forward to that!"

"Yeah. Great work, Joe. Tell the others. Great work. Grab as many as you can find."

"Will do." Joseph un-pocketed his own pack of cigarettes, lit one with the Zippo Bartley passed to him, passed it back.

"I always knew you were a fungi, Joe," Bartley said.

Joseph laughed smoke from his mouth and nose. "Yeah, well, good thing your cooking is better than your comedy."

Bartley took a last drag from his cigarette, rubbed it out with his shoe. "How's Ellen doing with the move this time?"

Joseph's head lowered, came back up. "Better. Better each time, I think. The panic is less extreme. It helps being, you know, with you all. I think her mind is... I think she's coping better."

"That's good, Joe."

"I'm just sorry that you all—"

"Joe. Don't be sorry. This existence is fucked up. She may be the most sane among us."

Joseph wiped one of his soil-smudged cheeks, rubbed his bald head. "Thanks, Bartley. Yeah, I know." He flicked the cherry off his cigarette into the dirt, licked his thumb to pat out the vestigial embers, slid it back into its pack. "Well, I'll go tell the others about the mushrooms. They'll be pumped that we got you cooking again."

Bartley didn't reply. He stared out at the camp, where many of the people stopped mid-action, their heads turning north, some speaking low to one another.

"Damn," Joseph said, his face now also turned north. "Gravedigger."

Bartley's eyes and head tracked that direction. He became more conscious of his Sig Sauer 1911 handgun's stainless steel profile pressing against the side of his left pectoral, the straps of its shoulder holster digging into his shirt.

Below the deep rich orange and pink that seeped into the late afternoon sky, Gravedigger and seven of his men moved through the wasted sweep of trees, toward the camp, their gait that of mercenaries—arrogance and relaxed discipline. Gravedigger walked out front, the others spread in a casual V-formation behind him. As they approached, Gravedigger's attention marked Bartley, and their trajectory shifted toward him.

"Go up and tell the others about the mushrooms," Bartley said without turning his head.

"You sure?" Joseph's eyes still followed the incoming group.

"Yeah. Don't worry."

"Okay, we're just up a short way. Shout if you need anything." And Joseph left.

As Gravedigger's group made their way around the perimeter of the camp and up the slope to Bartley, Bartley registered each of their faces. Some of them he had seen before.

Gravedigger's community called themselves the Keepers, self-proclaimed guardians of the peace in the new world, though Bartley and others in Bartley's camp had suspicions about the validity and ethics of their methods. The Keepers considered themselves the reestablishment of law, their power and judgement absolute, and they wore the garb of soldiers from various eras ranging from ancient to modern, which they scavenged from museums, private collections, and military compounds. In the contingent that now neared Bartley, a man they called Paladin wore a Medieval chainmail coat, a broadsword sheathed at his waist, a soot-black beard hiding the lower half of a scar that ran past his left eye. Another wore a Union Civil War jacket and a repurposed WWII paratrooper's chute pack. One of them, a quick-eyed man with a clavicle-length red beard whom Bartley recognized as the one called Wisecracker, wore a mix of the historical and the modern—an Old West style belt holster and revolver and a Kevlar vest.

Gravedigger, the Keepers' leader, now just several paces away from Bartley, wore what an archeologist might—khaki pants, a sweat-soiled brown leather jacket over a dirty off-white shirt buttoned down mid-chest. Looking late-fifties in age, he stood a sturdy six feet tall, his face with a short beard under blue eyes and a head balding back to its apex. Bartley's eyes moved to the long shovel slung across Gravedigger's back, its spade stained dark with rust and blood.

"Bartley, my good man," Gravedigger said as he stopped a few feet short of him, his voice warm but business-like, his men settling into at-ease stances behind him.

"John," Bartley said.

"How are the Samaritans doing this fine evening?"

"You know we don't call ourselves that."

"What?"

"The Samaritans. You know that."

"Yes, well, the named almost never name themselves, do they?"

"You named yourselves."

Gravedigger palmed his jawline. "I did say 'almost,' didn't I?"

Bartley looked past him into the tree-splintered distance. He wiped his forehead. The day seemed to be growing warmer as it ended. "How's the patrol going? No fouls, no harm, I hope." He instinctively glanced at the spade-end of Gravedigger's shovel.

"Yeah, well, glad you asked. You notice anything going missing from your camp?"

"Missing? No, but we haven't even been here a day. We're not even fully—"

"Because the Washington Clan—we stopped by earlier—they're missing some rations."

Bartley's head ticked to one side. "Rations. Really. Already."

"That's the word. They had six red coolers. They have five now."

"Sorry to hear that. But again, we haven't noticed any malfeasances yet."

"Noted. Now, on another matter, one of my guys back at camp has a wound that looks infected. You all have some antibiotics you could spare?"

"I'll talk to Marlene. She's our shot-caller when it comes to medical supplies. Is it bad?"

"No, not bad. Not yet. Nothing about to fall off. Just isn't getting any better."

"I'll talk to her soon. If we can spare it, I'll send a carrier over to your camp at first light tomorrow. You that way?" Bartley bladed his hand in the direction the small group of Keepers had come from.

"Yeah, almost dead-on," Gravedigger said.

"We'll always help if we can, John."

Gravedigger smiled. "That's why you're all called what you're called, Bartley."

Bartley shook his head.

"Ya'll Samaritans stay safe now. Need anything, just give us a holler."

The men behind Gravedigger stirred and turned to leave.

"We will, John."

Gravedigger pivoted and walked through his men, who waited for him to reach the lead before they all followed him back beneath the swelling colors of twilight.

Bartley tapped the side of his knee repeatedly, staring after them as they grew smaller with distance. He distractedly fingered the long scar that ran across the length of his forehead, rubbed the back of his hand against his beard groomed down to inches by Marlene with a dull pair of scissors. He looked to the camp, where people watching him went back to their previous activities. Shaking another cigarette from his pack to his mouth, he lit it, his lips pursing into the filter.

He looked again at the femur dropped from the world's barbaric randomness.

Wisecracker

Freddie "Jammer" Jamison, known now only as Wisecracker, watched as Paladin and Bouncer dragged a man from the thin dead line of brush amongst the burned forest, and dropped him into the ash and soot-dusted dirt at Gravedigger's feet. The man pushed himself up to his knees, spat earth-thickened saliva, his clothes darkened, tears running from his panic-globed eyes.

"No!" he shouted. "*No!* What are you going to do with me?"

Gravedigger, his chin still up, eyed the man with an amused scrutiny. "Well now, that all depends on you, little rabbit. Why were you hiding?"

"What?" The man, who appeared through the smeared layer of dirt on his face to be in his late thirties or early forties, shook his head in confusion.

"Why were you hiding? Over there, in the brush."

"I don't know you. I don't know any of you. I was scared." The man's tone implied that his answer was obvious.

Gravedigger's mouth flexed into a thoughtful frown, his head bobbing to one side.

"It's how I've survived this long," the man said. "We all know that. We all know that's how you survive in this shit-scape."

"And by stealing food?" Gravedigger said.

"What?"

"And by stealing the food you stole, right? If we all know these survival tactics of yours, then we know that, right?"

"What food? What are you talking about?" He glanced around at the eight men surrounding him.

"From a camp about a mile and a half yonder." Gravedigger motioned with his head.

Freddie saw understanding surface in the man's eyes—an understanding that he was in a situation different than what he originally thought, though just as dangerous.

"I don't know anything about that," the man said.

"Well I think you do, rabbit. I think that's why you were hiding. Why don't we start with a look into that pack on your back? Buckeye..." Gravedigger waved a finger at the Keeper known as Buckeye—an Ohio man wearing an antique raccoon-fur cap, buckskin jacket, and a sheathed foot-long bowie knife on his belt—who stepped toward the man and outstretched a hand.

The man coughed, spat again. He un-shouldered his backpack and placed one of the straps into Buckeye's hand.

Buckeye bunched the straps against the pack and handed it to Gravedigger, who dug through it briefly and tossed it aside.

"Why don't you just admit what you've done?" Gravedigger advanced toward the man.

The man, eyebrows lightninged in outrage and desperation, looked at his backpack, then back to Gravedigger. "What? You didn't find anything in there. You couldn't possibly have found anything in there!"

"Why, because you hid it somewhere else?"

"Because I didn't fucking take anything!"

"Admit it!" Gravedigger straightened. "Admit what you did. And we'll go easy." He shook his head. "Just admit it. We got you."

"Fucking witch-hunt. Fuck you."

Gravedigger kneeled down to the man's level. "Look, there's a decision you have to make here. See that man?" He looked over his shoulder.

The man's eyes followed.

One of the Keepers, a heavyset man with a belly-length brown beard, stepped forward. He wore an artificially aged metal replica of a Viking helmet, a chest plate from the Roman Empire, a fireman's hatchet on one hip and a butcher's cleaver on the other. He grinned and squatted like a shortstop between batter-ups.

"That's Lunchtime," Gravedigger said. "You know why we call him Lunchtime?"

The man began crying again, jolting sobs, mucus on his upper lip and strings of thick saliva at his mouth. He didn't answer.

"Because he eats anything. And he's always hungry." Gravedigger's voice softened, lowered. "So what do you think he's gonna do with you, rabbit? Just confess. And we'll go easy. Otherwise, you see that cleaver he carries? He's going to cut off your fingers and eat them in front of you like chicken wings." He leaned close, their faces inches apart. "What do you think?"

The man's sobs stilled, though his fear only seemed to sink deeper internally. His flickering bright green eyes, expelling large balled tears down his face, steadied as they met Gravedigger's. His jaw wrenched, his bite squeezing hard against words.

Wisecracker watched, knowing no words could save him.

"Confess!" Gravedigger shouted. "Confess and you'll receive mercy. Last chance, rabbit."

The man's entire body quaked, his face shaking tears loose into trembling trajectories from skin to earth. He held Gravedigger's stare.

"I confess," he said.

"There it is!" Gravedigger stood and widened his arms in celebration. "There it is!" He looked down at the man. "You confess?"

The man repeated, "I confess."

"Well, there you have it." Gravedigger looked around at his men. His gaze crossed Wisecracker's eyes for less than a second. "We have a guilty plea and the man is found guilty!"

He performed a circle of intermittent bows like a stage performer. He bowed toward Bouncer, Rockstar, Booster. His expression darkened. He shimmied the shovel around from his back to his hands.

"But, unfortunately, the plea came too late," he said.

Wisecracker looked at the shovel, looked down at the ground surrounding his own dirty Adidas.

Gravedigger continued, "Always best to begin with honesty. When we have to dig out the truth, well, that's not honesty at all."

The man, on his knees, his face gleaming with sweat and snot and spit, seemed dazed, his eyes looking past the group into the treacherous and unforgiving landscape ignited by the dazzling late morning sunlight.

Gravedigger had told the stories many times, about the shovel he carried with him from his previous life as a gravedigger in the old world. His family had owned a cemetery in Wisconsin, where they upheld the tradition of digging graves by hand.

"Sentence," Gravedigger said, "is death."

The man gave a soft cry before the first swing of the shovel connected with his head. He was dead after the second swing, but Gravedigger swung down a third time, the blade of the shovel's spade crunching through the already scrambled and spattered remains of skull and brain and skin.

A small smattering, three droplets of blood, showed in Wisecracker's window of vision, landing near his left sneaker. He heard cheering. He held his hands over his ears, closed his eyes. A few of the other Keepers slapped him on the back. One of them howled like a demented wolf.

A hand grabbed his right hand, peeled it back from his ear. Close hot breath made him recoil.

"You *love* it," the breath said.

Then the hand let go.

Christopher

Along the western perimeter of the Yellowstone clear zone, Christopher Smith sat in a faded red fold-out lawn chair in a small cluster of lodgepole pines untouched by disaster, dense enough to create a kind of seclusion. Periodically, he could hear the cannon-booms of thunder from the superstorm battering the landscape not far away. He took a large slurping bite of his canned noodle soup and looked up at his two companions—Terrance, a 35-year-old man, and Jeanie, a 74-year-old woman—both sitting in faded lawn chairs of their own, eating. They had been traveling with him for the past two clear zones.

Christopher's eyes narrowed on the man, two years younger than he was, flannel shirt with the sleeves rolled up, loose jeans and heavy boots, a beard thick around his wet chewing.

Terrance's eyes ticked up from his canned soup, met Christopher's.

"You got something you want to say?" Terrance said after a pause. His voice was deep and even.

"Yeah," Christopher said, his eyes flaring, "I do. I can't *believe* you left the gas can outside the car. Of all things, man. I mean, I'm trying to," he held up a palm, "but I just can't believe it."

Terrance sucked a drip of tomato soup off his thumb. "Me? I'm not the one that forgot to put it in the trunk."

"Let's not do this," Jeanie, said. Her creased features pleaded from within her fall of shoulder-length silver hair. "C'mon, you guys. This isn't going to solve a thing."

"I told you to put it in the trunk." Christopher's voice pitched up, volume heightened. "I told you! And we just drove right off without it. Left it sitting on the side of the road with a big red bow on it like some fucking idiots."

Terrance dropped his spoon into his soup, pointed a steady finger at Christopher. "You said 'Put the gas in the trunk' like you were saying 'I put the gas in the trunk.' Ain't my fault you didn't."

Christopher sat nodding to his own angry internal logic, glowering at Terrance, who started eating again. "You know you killed us, right? Without that gas, we're dead."

"Chris," Jeanie said.

"Well? Not like there's any fuel to find out here!" Christopher waved an arm, tilted his head.

Terrance dropped the spoon again, pointed the same finger. "You're just lucky our car is one of those hybrids. That's the only thing that might give us a chance of reaching the next clear zone. Then maybe you'll be able to sleep again at night."

"What do you mean 'our' car?" Christopher leaned forward. "I'm the one that found that car. Long before I met either of you."

Terrance shook his finger. "Watch your tone, Chris."

"Or what?" Christopher said. "You going to forget something else crucial to our survival?"

"Enough!" Jeanie said, her voice cutting through their attention. She lifted a shaky hand to adjust her large-rimmed glasses. "I have had enough of this. We don't need this right now. I don't need this right now. Isn't there enough crap in this world trying to kill us without us trying to kill each other? Isn't there enough worry about death without you declaring ours?" Her thin face quaked as she spoke. She sat with a dignified posture in a flowery blouse and a shin-length dress skirt, her back straight, her hands resting on her knees.

It ate at Christopher to see her upset.

He took a slow breath, dipped his head in concession. "Sorry, Jeanie. You're right. Of course."

In many ways, Jeanie reminded him of his mother.

He touched with his right hand the blue twine bracelet he wore around his left wrist. His mother had given it to him just a few years after the disasters began, when their luck with rummaging through pharmacies had evaporated, and she knew her medication was almost gone. After the medication ran out, she again suffered from schizophrenic hallucinations, growing more severe until one night she followed one of them straight into a massive thunderstorm. He had been sleeping, and woke too late to stop her. He caught up with her only in time to see her body lift from the ground and vanish into the dark swirling wind and rain and flashing jags of lightning.

"Yeah, sorry, Jeanie," Terrance said, and continued eating.

They sat in silence until Terrance tossed his empty can in the dirt and stood.

"I'm going to go for a walk," he said, "take a look around." He turned and strolled southeast through the trees.

Christopher, scraping the bottom of his own can, watched him leave.

"You know, I've known him longer than you have," Jeanie said. "He's a good man, Chris."

"Yeah, I'm not so sure about that," Christopher said.

"He is. And he feels bad about the gas. I can tell."

"Really? Because it seems like he's dumping that one on me."

"He's taking it hard is all. He has to deflect because the full weight of a mistake like that might be too much for him to bear right now, in all of this."

Christopher lowered his gaze, but she lowered her head to catch it.

"And he really doesn't need anyone else adding to that weight," she said. "Right?"

"Yeah, I get it, Jeanie. I'll ease up." He looked southwest, saw the distant glint of the silver Honda Accord parked just outside the tree cluster.

"Good. You're a good man too, Chris. It's this world that sets us against each other."

"Yeah, but wasn't it people like us who made this world what it is?"

"No," she said. "Not like us."

#

Christopher drove the final stake into the ground through the last loop along the bottom of the lime green nine-person tent while Terrance held the pole in place. Christopher tucked the hammer back in his canvas tool bag and zipped it shut. Both he and Terrance stepped back from the tent, looked it over.

"Looks good," Christopher said.

"Yup. Good work," Terrance said, dusting his hands against one another.

"You too."

"Looks great, boys," Jeanie said. She was sitting in her chair a few yards away, reading a crumpled copy of "Leaves of Grass" by Walt Whitman—one of Christopher's favorite books, though he didn't mention that to her.

"Alright," Christopher said. "You both can start moving your sleeping bags in. I left my chew in the car, so I'm going to make a quick run for it. I'll be back in—"

"No worries, man. I'll get it," Terrance interjected. "I have to go to the car anyway for my sunglasses. Center console right?"

"Yeah, but I got it. I'll grab your glasses too. I need a walk anyway." Christopher looked around the shaded area provided by the trees. "Where are your glasses? Glovebox?"

"Really, don't worry about it. Not sure where I left them, so I'll just go."

Christopher tilted his head in confusion, suspicion seeping into his brain. "I'll look for them."

"No need."

"Chris, just let Terrance go," Jeanie said. "He'll get your chewing tobacco."

Christopher looked from Terrance to Jeanie, back to Terrance.

"I'm going," Christopher said, and started walking.

He only made it twenty yards before Terrance jogged past and stepped in front of him.

"Chris, I said—"

"Why won't you let me go to the car, Terrance?"

"It's not that I won't—"

"What's going on? What did you do?" Christopher looked behind himself, saw that Jeanie had stood from her chair and walked a dozen paces toward them.

"It's nothing, Chris." He shrugged a half-smug concession. "I just, I left the car running so I could charge my iPod. I knew it'd piss you off. That's all."

Christopher blinked rapidly. Heat flooded his face. His breath came faster.

"You *what*? Hell yes that pisses me off! What the fuck are you thinking? And after you left the gas can? You're burning more gas for a fucking iPod?"

"I thought some music might do us all some good. It was for all of us."

Christopher's hand caved into a fist at his side.

Terrance added, "And it was you who forgot the tank."

The punch came quick, before Christopher realized he had thrown it, struck Terrance on the left hinge of his jaw and sent him backpedaling away. He bent over, both hands on the jaw joint.

"Chris!" Christopher heard Jeanie yell behind him, though he kept his eyes on Terrance, who recovered his stance and gazed in a rage back up at Christopher.

The left side of Terrance's face was already purpling. His mouth bent in a grimace.

In Christopher's periphery, he saw a fallen branch about the size of a small baseball bat near his feet. He went for it as Terrance charged, gripped it and swung it with both hands as he rose back up, just as Terrance reached him.

The branch caught Terrance in his left arm at the shoulder, unbalanced his forward inertia. He yelled and stumbled to Christopher's left, landing hard on his right shoulder in the dirt. His face locked in a wince. He sucked in air through his teeth, coughed from the stirred up earth.

Christopher pivoted, raised the branch again in case the fight continued, but felt a soft hand on his right arm. Jeanie was beside him, looking up at him.

"Chris, please stop," she said.

"You broke my fucking arm," Terrance yelled, and Christopher looked back to him. Terrance was rocking on the ground, holding his left shoulder with his right hand. He glared at Christopher. "What the hell, man? You break my arm?"

Christopher's stance softened. His shoulders sank. He dropped the branch.

#

Jeanie placed the collar of one of Terrance's spare shirts around his neck, pulled his left hand across through the right sleeve, and tucked the waist of the shirt under his elbow to create a makeshift sling as Christopher watched.

"My husband showed me this little trick once upon a time when I fell hiking," she said. "There you go. How does that feel?" She sat back in her chair.

Terrance, sitting in his chair, looked at Christopher, who was standing. "Like I have a broken arm."

"I'm sorry, Terrance. It shouldn't have gone that far," Christopher said.

"That's right," Jeanie said. "It shouldn't have. Now this little feud between you two needs to end. Now. Hard enough trying to survive; now we have one of us with a broken arm? It ends now, understand?"

Christopher nodded. "It's over."

"Easy for you to say, asshole," Terrance said.

"Terrance, stop." Jeanie looked from one of them to the other. "We let everything go. There's nothing to be gained from holding on to any of it. Now call a truce."

Terrance looked up at Christopher. "Truce," he said between squeezed teeth.

Christopher nodded again. "I'll go find some sticks for the fire."

"Good at finding sticks, aren't you?" Terrance said.

"*Terrance*," Jeanie said.

"Truce. Truce." Terrance held up his right hand.

As Christopher bent to gather sticks from the southern edge of their campsite, he heard the crunch of footsteps to the east.

"Easy," a voice said. "Easy now, we mean you no harm."

Christopher slowly turned his head to his left, saw three figures emerge from the trees. Two men and a woman, the lead man holding up a clip-fed hunting rifle. The others had similar rifles hanging from their shoulders. The woman also had a handgun holstered at her waist.

Christopher lifted his hands above his head.

"That's it. Real easy. We don't want to hurt you. Just want to talk." The three strangers stepped into the campsite, looked around, stood just ten yards from Christopher. "What's your name?"

"Christopher."

"Okay. Pleased to meet you, Christopher. I'm Joseph. This here is Tera, and that's Henry. We're just out on a scouting trip. We're foraging. But we don't steal. Okay? Understand what I'm saying?"

Christopher nodded, kept his hands raised. "Yeah."

"Okay," Joseph said. He lowered the rifle's barrel until it aimed at the ground. He looked toward the tent. "Where are the others?"

"What?"

"The other people. Besides you. You have three chairs set out. I'm asking because we might be able to help you all. That's all."

Christopher rotated his torso and looked at the campsite.

Terrance and Jeanie were both still sitting in their chairs by the tent. They stared at Christopher, their expressions hauntingly blank.

"They out in these trees somewhere?" Joseph said.

Christopher rotated back, his gaze emptying into the trees to the south, his mouth open, his eyebrows like soft razors. His arms dropped. Realization hit his shoulders and shoved him to his knees.

He thought of his mother. Her illness.

"Hey, you okay, friend?" Joseph stepped toward him.

Christopher's face collapsed into his hands and he began to cry. Sad, angry, grieving sobs.

"There are no others," he said. "It's just me."

Bartley and Marlene

As night stretched its descent, stars suffused the sky like a spill of lustrous dust, thousands of grains sized by depth and light, squeezing the ink between them. Marlene found Bartley sitting on a wooden stool outside the entrance of his tent, poking at a small fire with a long thin branch. He looked up as she neared, smiled.

"I was hoping you were still up," she said.

"Always am," he said. "You know me."

"Yeah. Today was a long one, though."

"Yeah. How's Charlotte?"

"Good. Asleep. Nora's looking after her. Mind if I sit?"

Bartley stood up, pushed his stool toward her, ducked into his tent and came back with another stool for himself. They both sat.

Bartley lit a cigarette, inhaled, passed it to her. She smiled and accepted, flicking it softly between her fingertips, took a drag and passed it back.

"Thanks," she said.

Bartley nodded.

"Can I ask, do you have any..."

Bartley reached into his jacket pocket, slid out a small silver flask, tossed it once lightly in his palm before holding it out to her.

"Thanks," she said again, took the flask.

"Wish it was better stuff. But it gets the job done."

She took a heavy drink, winced. "Tequila?"

He nodded.

"Not bad." She passed the flask back to him. He drank from it and screwed the cap back on.

"So how's it going with that guy they found?" she said. "You think he's okay?"

"Tough to say right now. Seems harmless. They said he was pretty distraught when they found him though. He's asleep now. Set up his tent on the south edge of camp. Henry's keeping an eye on him."

"Distraught?"

"Yeah, broke down and started crying pretty hard apparently. Joseph said that he… I guess he stares off. At nothing. Like he's looking at something no one else can see. You should probably take a look at him first thing tomorrow."

"Sure. Just have him come by the infirmary tent."

"Thanks." He passed the cigarette to her. She took another drag.

He glanced up at her profile as she smoked, her face playing in the shadow and light from the fire. He was in love with her, though he filed that away to an un-lived life, as if it was an echo from some parallel reality. He lived *here*, but kept *there* in the hopeless back pocket of his heart. That is how he coped. That is how he lived every day.

"You see Ellen today?" he said.

"Yeah. She's pretty much the way she is after every move. I gave her some L-theanine, but that's not much help in her state. If anything, I'm hoping it'll have a placebo affect." She took another drag and passed the cigarette back to him. "I'm reluctant to give her anti-depressants because we don't have many and once they run out she might be worse off."

"Yeah, that's rough."

He handed her the flask again and she took another drink, smaller this time.

"That's good," she said, handing it back to him.

"Yeah, it gets better with each sip."

She laughed. "You know, that soup you made earlier was pretty damn delicious. A popular opinion from what I heard."

"Thanks." He twisted the low burning cigarette between his thumb and forefinger.

"Seriously, Bartley. It lifted the mood of the entire camp. We needed that."

He smiled, looked into the fire. They sat in silence a moment.

"Do you ever think that's it?" he said, eyes still on the fire. "A cold drink and a hot meal? That really, when it boils down to it, little else matters? At least before and after you digest the meal and grow thirsty again. That all the shit about good and bad and clean and dirty and joy and pain and being remembered or forgotten, that all of it is an afterthought to food when you're hungry and drink when you're parched? Is that why there's that final meal on death row? Did they tap into something there, something deep in the human condition? I mean, is there right and wrong, or is there just fed and starving?"

She stared at him, smiled after a few seconds. "No, I don't think that. You know why?"

He looked at her.

"Because I know you," she said, her eyes holding to his. She paused, looked away. "I think there's greed, and I think there's sacrifice, and the people between." She cleared her throat, smiled again and reached a hand to his knee. "Goodnight, Bartley. Thank you for the drink."

She stood, and vanished slowly from the firelight.

Marlene and Christopher

Marlene watched Christopher cautiously as he sat in a metal folding chair just inside the raised canvas of the infirmary tent, which was located close to the center of camp in order to protect the medical supplies the group had scavenged and stockpiled. Christopher's head was turned left, and despite the bustling of the camp's late morning activity, he gazed bleakly at the undecorated rear material of a nearby tent. Henry, who had escorted Christoper to the infirmary, had offered to stay as protection, but she declined in an effort to make her new patient more comfortable, more trusting.

"Christopher," Marlene said.

Christopher looked back to her.

"Did you hear what I asked you?"

His eyes flickered around the inside of the infirmary tent. He scratched his upper arm and shook his head.

"I asked why you were so upset when Jospeh and the others found you."

He took a reactionary breath. "I... I don't know." His hands began rubbing the top of his thighs.

"You don't know?"

He shook his head as if he didn't believe himself. "No."

"Christopher. I'm here to help you. But I can't if you don't tell me what's going on."

His features flexed in conflict.

"You can trust me," she said.

He looked back to the rear of the tent. She looked too.

"They said you've been staring. Staring at nothing like there's something there."

His eyes moved back to her.

"Do you see something, Christopher?"

He stared at her for a few long seconds. "People," he said.

"You see people."

"Two of them. Jeanie and Terrance."

"They have names."

"They're standing there right now, by that tent." He pointed to where he had been looking, shook his head.

Marlene instinctively looked again. "There's no one by that tent."

"That's right. At least, not that anyone else can see."

"So you're having hallucinations?"

"My mom had them. She was.... she was schizophrenic."

"So you think you have your mother's illness?"

"I don't know, miss. What do you think?" He visibly tensed. "I didn't even know. I didn't even know they weren't there. That they weren't real. Not until your people showed up and couldn't see them. I had been traveling with them for months. God." His jaw trembled with emotion; she could see its muscles bite against it.

"Okay. It's okay, Christopher. It's not your fault." She leaned forward. "Breathe, try to stay calm. From my understanding, these hallucinations can be brought on and exacerbated by stress. It's a wonder these symptoms didn't manifest sooner."

"Yeah, well. So what am I going to do now, miss? Without medication, I mean, my mom..."

Marlene held up a hand. "Hey, good news. Coincidentally enough, antipsychotics are one thing we have a decent supply of. I think they're the right kind." She stood and walked over to a row of large brown trunks, looked at their labels, opened one.

"Guess you haven't had anyone as crazy as me," Christopher said.

"Guess not." She turned with a jar-sized plastic container in her hand and smiled reassuringly at him. "You're not crazy, Christopher. You have a condition. And from what you told me about your mother, it's genetic." She walked over to the table in the center of the tent, began sorting the pills into a small white glossy pill container. "Like I said, we have a decent amount. At least enough to get you to the next clear zone or two. And who knows what we'll find then?"

"Exactly. Who knows?"

She tore a piece of paper from a small pad on the desk, scribbled down dosing directions and folded it. "Look. We aren't going to give up on you, okay? That's not what this group does." She walked over to him as he stood. "You're with good people now. There's hope. Okay?"

She handed him the small pill container and the piece of paper.

Christopher nodded. "Thank you," he said.

"You can trust me. Let me know if there's anything else I can do."

Christopher turned to leave.

"And, Christopher."

He turned back.

"You should always be honest with me," she said.

He nodded again, and left the tent.

On his way back to his own tent, he looked over his shoulder. Behind him and one aisle of tents over to his left, he saw Jeanie and Terrance walking slowly, following him, their expressions almost sad.

Christopher stopped, rattled the pills in their container, and unfolded the directions.

Bartley

Thunder woke Bartley to a start, his eyelids shuttering in the night, hands searching immediate and aimless over the cross-textured polyester tent floor. Fat heavy slaps of rain against the upper tarp built like a swelling applause, sped to a crescendo, sound colliding with itself until each drop became indiscernible from the others. His retinas spasmed in a strobe of lightning chased by another sequence of booms like bombs felt in the skeleton. Bartley panicked, wondered how this had happened. Wondered who was helming the radios.

It's too close, he thought. *It's already here.*

He couldn't locate his gun or his pack, just saw barren inner canvas around him in an illuminant lash of lightning.

This is it, he thought. *It's happening. The worst is here.*

Within another splash of light, he dove forward on his knees, found the small metal zipper to the entrance, peeled it down, stepping up into the freezing and overwhelming barrage of downpour, water knuckling against him. He looked up, looked back down, raised a forearm to his face, almost couldn't see or breathe through the rain's relentless onslaught. He lifted his head to survey what he could of the camp.

The rows of tents flapped madly and bent to the tempest, the aisles between them dark and reflective from mud and water shimmering with the impact of raindrops. He couldn't see anyone in the aisles or stirring in the tents. He hoped they had gone. He hoped they had already evacuated the grounds.

His clothes were hanging wet and icy against his skin. He looked in the direction where the vehicles were parked, saw nothing in the distance's dark. He sprinted through the cross sections of aisles toward Marlene's tent, his feet plunging and sliding in the water-mucked earth.

"Marlene!" he shouted over the roar of the rain as he reached her tent. He fumbled with the outer zipper, his fingertips cold and numbing. "Marlene, you and Charlotte okay? Marlene!"

He managed to grip the zipper and ripped it upward in a sweeping arc, pushed down the entrance flap.

The tent was empty. Completely. Not even their belongings remained.

Bartley turned toward the vehicles, turned again when he heard a high-pitched scream almost drowned by the thrum of the storm.

Thirty yards away, toward the center of camp, Charlotte stood center-aisle, screaming, immobilized by fear, her hair sopped down over her face and shoulders, her small body shaking in the cold.

He ran toward her.

"Charlotte!"

"Bartley!" she yelled when she heard his voice.

He lifted her from the mud and water, carried her.

"Where's your mom?"

"I don't know."

Charlotte was crying. He could feel her trembling and convulsing in his arms.

"Okay. We have to get to the vehicles. Okay? It'll be okay."

He ran with her, the hitch in his stride from the old gunshot wound in his left thigh more pronounced.

He reached the east perimeter of camp. The vehicles were gone.

"That, that doesn't make sense," he said. "She wouldn't leave you."

"What's happening? What's wrong?" Charlotte said.

"She would never leave you." He looked over at the nearby knot of lodgepole pines, looked up at their thin canopy lit by a volley of lightning, giant forks of energy like electric hands reaching out, as if the storm itself was asking Charlotte from his arms.

Bartley tried to yell, his voice bottled in his throat.

He saw an airplane flying distant in the sky, just a prong of light in the night, the sonic whoosh of its engines following it through the storm.

Bartley tried again to yell—to curse the plane, to ward off the bright monstrous hands reaching for the small girl. Desperation rushed in his chest.

When his voice finally broke through—like a dam collapsing—it was a belting yell, and between the worlds of consciousness he felt a freedom.

He awoke sitting upright at the tail-end of his yell, his shirt heavy with sweat against him, morning light warming his tent. He breathed. The outline of a shadow appeared at the entrance.

"Bartley?" a female voice called from outside.

"Yeah," he said.

He watched the tent's zipper slide open in a half-parabola.

Marlene's face appeared in the opening. "Hey." She looked down at the dark V of sweat running down his shirt. "Bartley—you okay?"

"Yeah, fine." He was glad she hadn't heard him yell. "What's up?"

"We have newbies incoming." She cocked her head southwest.

"Got it." Bartley picked up his shoulder holster and hooked each arm into its straps. Marlene backed away from the entrance and he exited the tent and walked with her triple-speed among the tents, noticing a quiet buzz in the camp as the news whispered through it.

As Bartley and Marlene reached the southwest perimeter, they found Henry, Nora, and Tera armed and waiting, and Bartley immediately spotted the newcomers, three slow-moving figures approaching in the bright morning, just fifty yards out along the edge of the volcanic plateau, two men and a small boy.

Bartley walked out to meet the strangers roughly fifteen yards from the nearest line of tents, the others following him. He raised a hand in greeting.

"Hello there," he said.

The two men appeared to be middle-aged, the boy about five or six years old.

"Greetings," one of the men said. "We come in peace. My name is Whitman. This is my brother, Xavier, and his son, Mercer. We're pleased to make your acquaintance."

"Hello," Xavier said. A constellation of scars that looked like his skin had met with a cheese grater marked the right side of his face. He placed his hands on the boy's shoulders.

"Hi," Mercer said.

Bartley nodded, smiled at the boy, introduced himself and the group members with him.

Whitman nodded to each of them. "We've been observing your camp for a while now, from a distance. What we can tell, you seem like our type of people. Good people. We thought we'd introduce ourselves."

Bartley kept an unassuming expression. "Okay."

He observed the strangers' appearances. They were surprisingly clean and well-groomed, both men with beards shaped to their faces, the boy's hair neatly cut. All three of them wore backpacks, the boy's with a likeness of Mickey Mouse stitched to it. Bartley saw no weapons.

"How are you all traveling?" he said.

Whitman glanced over his right shoulder. "We have a vehicle back there, just past that elevation. A Jeep Compass. Still in pretty good condition. We have a decent amount of gas and water. We're low on food. Thought we'd approach you all on foot first. Didn't want to startle you fine people."

"We appreciate that," Bartley said. He looked at Henry to his left, at Nora to his right, back to the newcomers. "Okay, well, I think we should all sit down and have a chat. Come on, let's talk over a meal. You all hungry?"

Whitman smiled. "Starving."

Joseph

Joseph set his backpack down on his cot, zipped it shut. He could peripherally see his wife watching him from where she stood on the opposite side of their annoyingly orange five-person tent.

"Do you ever think of our daughter, Joseph? Do you?"

"Every day, Ellen." His response was automatic. "In fact, I don't think there's ever a moment I'm not thinking of her. Now come on. Calm down."

"Calm down? You know I hate when you say that. And how can I calm down when she is only in our heads? Do you get that?" She pointed from herself to him. "Our heads. No one else's. If we die, that's it. That's the end of her. She lives only in our minds now. We have to take care of ourselves."

"Yeah, I get that, Ellen. I think she is here though, and she's with us whether we're alive or dead. And when we die, we'll still be with her. And we'll see her waiting for us."

Ellen tossed her head to clear strands of shoulder-length brown hair from her face. She interlinked her arms at her chest. "What will I do without you?" She switched her argument. "You go out on these... these things too often. It's too much."

Joe reached under his cot and lifted his black Remington bolt-action hunting rifle from the floor of the tent.

"It's for the camp, Ellen. There's a lot of area out there to cover. We go through this every time a move is fresh."

"But why do *you* have to go?"

"You know why."

"But every trip?"

"Look," he let the stock of the rifle drop to rest on the cot, holding it with one hand like a staff. "I don't have to go on them at all. And I've told you: you want me to stay and I'll stay. I won't go. But this is what I do, Ellen. This is what makes me feel useful. Like I'm contributing something to these people."

Ellen's eyes unfocused, lowered. "I don't contribute."

"You do. To me. To us. The whole camp loves you, is behind you. And you're behind me. And I love you."

Her eyes refocused on him. "Be careful out there," she said.

"I always am." He threaded his arms into the backpack, checked the safety on the rifle and shouldered it. He looked at her. "Always. You going to be okay?"

She smiled obligingly, unconvincingly. "Yes."

He nodded, smiled with the most reassurance he could summon to his face, and left the tent.

Outside the air was bright with the sun and the dirt was dry at his feet, the sweetness of pine and the illusion of summer simmering in his nostrils. The dim shade and shadow of his tent —which seemed to cling to him with a dragging gravity—dried up and flaked from his shoulders as he walked, as he grew further from the darkness he would not even acknowledge to himself. He smiled, nodded, even winked at some of his fellow camp members as he passed them outside their tents, shaking hands, squeezing short hugs, speaking promises to a poker game or a night with a pieced-together board of Monopoly. His steps fell crisp and feathery.

As he reached the group's garden, he saw Michael rearranging its plants, pulling pots and troughs of sprouting soil from the light into the shade beneath a 4-legged canopy tarp. Michael straightened and brushed his hands together, took a quick measurement by lining up his arm, hand bladed, with the angle of the sun's trajectory. His mouth arced with a satisfied head-tilt.

"How're they looking?" Joseph said, placing a hand on one of the canvas poles.

Michael turned and smiled. "Oh, hey, Joe." He looked back to the plants. "Healthy. Very healthy. Just getting their positions timed right. The tomatoes are really coming in. Good to get everything back out in the sun. Those trips in the van always make me nervous. And these squash, these squash are absolutely singing. Growing like grass." He pointed to a dense row of giant leaves and stems twisting over the edges of their soil bed, littered with bright orange flowers and bumpy yellow bulbs. "I mean, they aren't the kind we thought they were, but they're edible. Don't let the warts fool you."

"Everything looks great," Joseph said, ignoring the mention of warts.

"Yeah." Michael bobbed his head, still admiring the plants like a new father. "Not too bad at all."

"Tera around?"

"Should be back here any minute now. She was watching the kid for Marlene. I know you all have another trek planned."

"Yeah."

Michael turned from his plants. "Well, garden's doing well, so don't put too much pressure on yourselves."

"Right." Joseph looked absently back across camp toward his tent. "Yeah, no. Sometimes it's just good to get out there. See what we can find."

Michael's eyes followed Joseph's, then moved back to the forager's face. "Hey, let Ellen know that I'd love her help here anytime. Easy work. But important. Just as soon as she's ready, yeah?"

Joseph snapped free from his attention's pull. "Yeah. I will. Thanks, Michael."

#

Joseph, Tera, and Henry walked shoulder-aligned a few feet apart through an open stretch of burnt and broken tree trunks north of their camp, their boots softly chewing soot-swept dirt. Further to their north, a narrow score of trees rivered up and across a shallow rise of land where, just beyond its crest, the Keepers had nested their camp, and the three foragers gradually shifted their direction east, each of their rifles shouldered, their movements casual but careful.

Joseph thumbed his rifle's strap.

"So how are things with you and Michael?" he said. "Seems like you two are getting along."

"Yeah," Tera said. "Yeah, Michael's great. Things are going really great between us." She smiled, keeping her eyes on her steps. "It's nice."

"He's a good man."

"He is."

"And he's a magician with that garden," Henry said. "We're going to have to start calling him the plant-whisperer."

Tera laughed. "Yeah, he sure knows that garden alright." She looked at Joseph. "How about you, Joe? How are things with you and Ellen?"

"Oh, you know. Things are always tough around a move. But she's...

we're good. Getting through it."

"That's good. Michael told me he asked her to help in the garden."

"Yeah." Joseph stepped around a massive tangle of upturned roots that clutched clods of dark soil speckled through with the tiny ends of their own tendrils. "That was nice of him."

"Well, I'm sure he could use the help. Do you think it would help her?"

"I do," Joseph said. "Wouldn't put money on her taking him up on it though. We'll see."

They moved toward an undulation along the eastern base of the slope that rose up to the Keepers' camp.

"Henry, what's going on with that—" Joseph started.

"*Look*!" Henry breathed, eyes speared ahead, a pointed finger aligning with them.

Thirty yards into their path, where the earth bowled into a low crown of fallen branches and a side-turned tree trunk, Jospeh could see a pair of large brown wings periodically rising in spasming flaps from behind the dismantled tree's dark array.

"A bird," Tera said.

"A big damn bird by the look of it," Joseph said. "Has to be a hawk or an eagle."

As they walked closer, their sightline of the bird cleared; the animal was large, about three feet in height, with a long fanned tail, dark brown torso, and gilded feathers running down the back of its head.

"A Golden Eagle," Joseph said. He un-shouldered his rifle slowly, held it with both hands at his waist. He could barely recognize the eagle due to its starved condition—its frame frail, almost skeletal, with featherless patches on its torso and at the top of its right wing where the skin underneath showed a glistening red. "It's in bad shape."

"What's it doing? What's got it so crazy?" Tera said.

"The fuck is that? Aw, shit," Henry said, placing a hand on the top of his head.

As the group stepped within five yards of the dip in the land, they could all see the body—dead, male—the crazed eagle tearing at the pale blue flesh at the neck with the dagger-like tip of its downturned beak. Half of the dead man's face had already been stripped to the raw red underneath. An eye was missing. The other eye, lid gone, aimed stilly upward, the chilling certainty of an unflinching pupil like a soul frozen.

Joseph rested the rifle on his collar bone with his right hand, put the back of his left hand against his nose and mouth.

The smell of decay's inception. Blood, but not running. Volcanic-black hair stiffly twisted with dried mud and baked air. Joseph guessed the window for the time of death was one to two days. He looked to the half of the man's face that was still intact, down to the buckskin jacket now spattered with blood and soil.

"It's Buckeye," he said.

"The Keeper?" Henry leaned in, studying the face, the garb beneath it. "Yeah, that's him."

Joseph bowed his chin and eyelids.

"Damn," Tera said.

The eagle's wings blossomed again, their width as wide as a grown human's height, its razored beak pulling again and again at the already molted section of face, gooey red strings of tissue developing between the repeated strikes. Another yank from the bird's feeding rotated the dead Keeper's head to the left.

Joseph's eyelids narrowed, pinched, blinked. He stepped closer while the others stayed back.

"You see that?" he said. "Just above the right ear." He bent his knees and lowered himself toward the head. "It's a bullet wound."

#

When the foragers arrived back at the Samaritans' camp, Joseph separated from the others to search for Bartley to inform him about the body. He strode through the camp's aisles in the mid-afternoon light, dodging the eyes of other camp members as he passed them. As he turned within vision of Bartley's tent, he could see the simmer of a dying fire at its entrance, Bartley and Gravedigger standing on either side, opposing postures, talking.

Bartley looked past Gravedigger at Joseph approaching.

"Joe," Bartley said, "you're back early. Everything okay?"

Gravedigger turned to Joseph, his eyes pitching upward in a roll, his lips flexing and stretching flat into his cheeks, irritated by the interruption.

"Tera, Henry, we're okay, Bartley," Joseph said. He looked at the Keeper. "You need to hear this too, Gravedigger." He didn't hesitate, looking from one man to the other as he spoke. "We found a body. Buckeye's. Just down the slope from the Keepers' camp. Shot in the head by the looks of it."

"By the looks of it?" Gravedigger said.

"Yes," Jospeh said. "I'm sorry."

Bartley's eyes moved to Gravedigger. "You don't seem surprised, John."

Gravedigger's eyes were still on Jospeh. "What gave it away? The bullet hole in his fucking head?" He looked at Bartley. "Of course I'm not surprised. We found him yesterday. Son of a bitch shot himself. Suicide, clear as day."

Joseph's eyebrows bunched. He looked from Gravedigger to Bartley.

"Shit," Bartley said. His eyes flashed toward Joseph, but stayed on the Keeper. "Why didn't you bury him, John?"

Gravedigger smiled with a mocking disgust. He held up a finger. "Because we don't bury quitters, Bartley. Buckeye wanted to punch out. That's on him. Fucking coward if you ask me." He looked at Joseph. "Thanks for the insight, detective. Now, if you fellas will excuse me, I have more rounds to make. Good talking with you, Bartley." He turned from the Samaritans, and walked toward the edge of their camp.

Joseph watched him leave. "He came alone this time?"

Bartley nodded. "He did."

"Strange reaction to Buckeye."

"Yeah. Well. He's a strange guy."

"Doesn't quite fit though. The suicide I mean."

Bartley looked at Joseph. "You think Gravedigger took out one of his own men?" There was no judgment or rhetoric in the question.

"I don't know. But the bullet hole, it doesn't look like a pointblank shot." Joseph's hands raised and motioned to measure a scene only he could see. "I've been around a suicide before, unfortunately. Found the body right after it happened." His eyes unfocused from Gravedigger into an empty gaze. In his mind, he saw his daughter. "This didn't seem like that. There's something about this that just doesn't add up. I can't quite nail it down, and Buckeye's body was moved so it's tough to say for sure, but," he paused, almost as if to outlive the gravity of his conclusion, "I don't think this was a suicide, Bartley. Not at all."

The Sown

Henry stepped forward among the other campers to the banquet-length trio of fold-out tables in the camp's garden, and looked down at the plates of freshly sliced vegetables and fruit. Michael, the camp's gardener, had decided to put out a generous sampling of the garden's first harvest—an event to buoy morale. Fervent chatter busied the air around the tables as avid hands reached to pluck from the bounty.

Henry's hand lowered to a plate bright with large thick-cut wafers of ripe tomatoes. The fruit was still cool and wet from the canopy's shade as he lifted a slice to his face. He held it briefly under his nose, inhaled, then bit into it, the tomato's flesh bursting with liquid between his teeth, the refreshing acidic zest pinning his senses into a conflux. His eyebrows pinched, raised, eyes shut, opened to look down at the half-eaten red circle between his fingers. He backed away from the table, away from the crowd of other campers, still chewing, turned and walked slowly through the avenues of the camp. He took another bite, half of the half that was left, and again his eyes closed.

He remembered his grandmother's garden behind her house in Omaha when he was just a boy. Tomatoes and basil and strawberries and oregano and parsley and so many other plants, all enclosed by a white picket fence with paint so textured he could touch it with his sight. And he remembered, when the tomatoes were ripe, he could bite into them like an apple, and he did, juice running onto his shirt, his mother lamenting the stains and his grandmother joking that he was worse than the wild gophers and rabbits. And as Henry put the last bite of the tomato slice into his mouth, he wasn't just remembering those moments, he was living in them.

He walked among the tents in a daze, readjusting the rifle slipping from his shoulder, the camp's rows coasting past him in a dull multicolored collage. His right boot-tip hiccuped against a stone. He sucked on the fingertips that had been holding the tomato, wiped them on his jeans as he emerged on the far west perimeter of the camp. He walked up the slight slope to the front line of a small stretch of trees and sat on a side-resting trunk of a lodgepole pine.

Henry interrogated his teeth with his tongue, swallowed the tomato's last shadow, and patted down his right jacket pocket, searching for and and finding his cherry-brown Briarwood pipe, his other hand fetching the small plastic gas-station bag of tobacco from the left. He peeled the bag open gingerly, pinched the stale and low-quality product into his pipe, and stuffed it down deeper with his right forefinger, pressing and lifting in alternation with short quick puffs at the mouthpiece. Satisfied with the airflow, he fingered a loose match from his breast pocket and struck it lit with his thumbnail, puffing shortly and repeatedly as he held its flame gently to the pipe's bowl, the tobacco catching slowly to cherry underneath the focus and reflection in his eyes. He took a long draw and let the smoke wallow from his jaw.

Caleb, one of the younger adults in the camp at 22 years old, hair cut close to his scalp and an optimism dilating his face, walked by along the camp's perimeter, on his security rounds. The young man had his old-school lever-action Winchester strapped behind his right shoulder.

He grinned at Henry as he passed. "*Henry*," he stretched out the name in a friendly growl.

"How goes it, kid?" Henry said.

"You know. Another day in paradise."

Henry chuckled outwardly. Inwardly, he didn't. He watched Caleb continue along the outer rows of tents.

Henry took another toke, blew a cloud, absently scratched a silvering sideburn. Whenever he observed the younger members in camp, he recognized the pull of jealousy with which the old viewed the young. An irrational concept, he knew, people feeling bitter over a thing they once possessed, a coin they had palmed and spent. Like eating a sandwich and watching resentfully as the next person ate theirs. One generation lived their allotted years, then the next one did. Only linearity, the inevitable procession of time, created indignity. And even beyond that, he felt sympathy for the young. In the present days darkened by tragedy and devastation, the older a person was, the more of the old world they had experienced, the less of the new. That ratio favored the aged.

He looked down through the smoke of another pipe hit, at his left hand, the wedding ring that lingered long past his happiness. His thumbnail ran through one of the ring's tungsten grooves.

His mouth side-saddled. He flexed the fingers on his left hand. The knuckles were chapped and cracking from the swings in climate. He bit into the pipe. He smoked. The smell of burning tobacco and warm air and soil and tree bark surrounded him.

The faint notes of a child's laugh drifted from the trees behind Henry. He turned an ear toward the sound. A child's voice speaking words he couldn't discern. He stood and walked in its direction, taking another draw from his pipe.

About twenty yards into the tree line, he spotted Mercer, the young boy that had arrived with the newcomers. The child weaved back and forth through the trees, running, skipping, chittering a narration of his own imaginary adventures, occasionally stopping to kick at the dry orange-brown needles on the forest floor.

Henry smiled, tapped out the tobacco in his pipe and ground out the embers with the forefoot of his boot sole. His smile turned as his eyes focused in on the top of the boy's head, on an adult-sized raccoon-fur cap that kept slipping down over the boy's eyes as he ran and skipped and jumped. A cap Henry recognized.

It was Buckeye's, the Keeper they had found dead just a few days before.

Henry's heart rushed. His right foot stepped back.

Mercer looked up and saw him. The boy stopped.

"Hi," Mercer said.

"Hey there, Mercer. How's it going today, bud?" Henry tried to keep his voice calm, friendly. He stepped toward the child.

"Good," Mercer said. "I'm an explorer."

"I can see that. Got the hat and everything. Very cool."

Mercer's eyes flashed upward. He took the hat from his head, held it in his hands.

"Where'd you get a cool hat like that, anyway?" Henry said.

"My dad said I could have it. But I wasn't supposed to be wearing it yet." The boy's eyes emanated guilt, fear. "He said he'd tell me when I could."

"Ah, is that so?" Henry kept his voice casual. He stepped again toward the boy.

"Yeah. You aren't going to tell him, are you?" Mercer's voice was pleading.

"No, no. I won't tell him. Your secret's safe with me." Henry held out a hand. "Can I see the hat real quick though, pal? Promise I'll give it right back."

Henry heard the crackle of breaking pine needles, looked to his right.

Xavier stood just over ten yards away among the trees.

Henry—a skilled hunter and marksman who had taught many of the Samaritans how to shoot fast and accurately—didn't even have time to turn his rifle before Xavier's handgun was up and aimed, and a bullet's heat tore through Henry's mind.

#

Bartley drank from the whiskey bottle, jeweled by firelight, straightened it out toward Joseph, who palmed it with his eyes not leaving Bartley's tent-front blaze, around which they both sat. Jospeh let out a stressed breath and drank.

Bartley's vision began to bend from the alcohol. He sucked on a half-smoked cigarette, stamped a thumb and forefinger into his eyes. They came away wet.

He looked at Joseph across the fire, its light brightening his irises.

Henry was dead.

When the shot had sounded earlier that day—a sharp pop rippling through the camp, its echoing bass chasing—Bartley had just reached the camp's garden for the harvest sampling. Some of the campers had panicked. Others had moved toward the sound instinctively, as Bartley had, his mind's momentum unconsciously shoving him into a run. When he had reached the trees, a small gathering already surrounded the body. Caleb was among them, chanting frantically that he had been the first to the scene. Henry's blood was on Caleb's clothes, the deceased man's head pulled up on Caleb's knees. The young man stared around fiercely, eyes begging. Bartley recognized the shock.

Now, looking from Joseph to the campfire, replaying the scene in his mind, Bartley stifled a rising nausea.

Safety was not attainable in this world, no matter preparation or perceived protection—a fact already proven, though the day's incident incited a reminder.

Joseph passed the bottle back with an audible swallow, fanned a hand to show he was done. His palms on his knees helped him stand. He raised his face to the late evening sky, looked down across the dimming horizon of tent tops.

"What was he doing out there, Bartley?" he said. "I mean, I saw him at the harvest. Just minutes…must have been just minutes before."

"I don't know," Bartley said, his left hand twisting against the smooth neck of the bottle.

They had been retreading this discourse since the fire was lit.

"Yeah, well," Joseph lashed a hand lazily in a finishing gesture. "I'm going to head out. I don't want Ellen to worry. See you at sunrise?"

Bartley nodded. "Yeah."

Security around the camp had been immediately increased after Henry's body had been found. Bartley and Joseph's next patrol began at sunlight's earliest incision.

Joseph's head bobbed in acknowledgment, slowed and pivoted into a disbelieving shake as he turned and walked west, up the gradually rising aisle toward his and his wife's tent.

Despite the sickness that hung in Bartley's gut, his thoughts again encored the day's horrendous event—the sequence surrounding the shot, the body's discovery—wringing his memory for every detail. The faces, the bodies, their positioning and posture. Perceived purpose. Reaction. Timing.

He was sure he had missed something.

His eyes searched the unforgiving fire, closed one eyelid to iron out his vision. He flicked his cigarette into the flames, looked up at the star-packed sky. Its vastness calmed him, made human problems seem less suffocating. He breathed a stress-shaken breath.

"Charlotte!" He heard Marlene's voice just seconds before he heard children's footsteps growing closer. Charlotte and Mercer burst out from the row of tents opposite Bartley and into the aisle just a few yards from his campfire.

Bartley knew Marlene was upset when she used her daughter's full first name.

Charlotte turned toward the direction of her mother's voice. "Yeah, Mom!"

"Get back here right now! I told you not to leave my sight! With everything we talked about today?" Marlene's voice rattled with anger and worry. Frustration.

"Coming, Mom! Sorry!" Charlotte sighed, turned and noticed Bartley. "Hey, Bartley." She looked at Mercer. "Sorry, Mercer, I have to go. My mom's mad. I'll see you later." She bolted back between tents toward the inner area of the camp.

Mercer stood watching her go, then turned to Bartley. "Hey, Bartley."

"Hey there, Mercer," Bartley said. "How's it going?"

"It's going good." Mercer stepped closer to the fire.

"That's good. How are you? How're you, your dad, and your uncle settling in? You like it here?" Bartley glanced around, expecting Xavier or Whitman to show up looking for their boy. Especially after the events of the day. He saw only tents and shadows.

"Yes. I like it here a lot. I hope we can stay."

"Well, that's the plan, Mercer. We all like having you here. Charlotte's glad to have a buddy, I'm sure. And your dad and uncle seem like good people."

"Yeah, they are. I just wish they didn't goodbye people."

Bartley's eyebrows lowered. "Goodbye people? You guys leave other people a lot?"

"Yeah. Well, no. They make people go away. From here. I wish they didn't." Mercer stared into the shadows. "I've asked them to not."

Bartley watched the boy's face. "From here?"

Mercer looked at Bartley. "From life."

Bartley's gut twisted, his jaw muscles flexing as he bit back his initial reaction. Mercer seemed to detect the reaction anyway.

"I need to get back to my dad," he said.

Bartley couldn't suppress the question rising in his throat, though he tried to keep his voice regular. "Mercer, did they have anything to do with what happened today? Did they—"

"I have to get back. See you later, Bartley." Mercer turned and sprinted away before Bartley could ask again.

Bartley leaned forward into a stupefied silence.

His mind ran circles. Xavier had been in the small group of people around Henry's body when Bartley had arrived at the scene. Thinking back, Bartley had looked up from the body to see Xavier had been staring at him. Bartley thought nothing of it at the time, but it was as if Xavier was reading him. Gauging something.

Bartley stood, catalyzed by a crescendo of emotional momentum, but a gun hammer's metallic click stopped him solid.

Whitman emerged from the shadows across the aisle, a 10mm pistol held low, at the his waist, the squarish barrel squared at Bartley. Whitman's expression was dead, his eyes unreadable.

"Easy there, Bartley," he said. "I don't want to shoot my way out of this camp, but I will if I have to." He looked over his shoulder. "Kids, right? Always keeping us honest."

"What do you want," Bartley said.

"I'll start with your gun. Nice and slow. Put it on the ground and kick it to me." Bartley drew his 1911 pistol from its shoulder holster, kept it aimed down, its handle toward Whitman. He considered turning it, firing, but there were too many people nearby, quiet in their tents. He couldn't risk a gunfight. And he thought of Buckeye, and he thought of Henry—one of the most knowledgeable weapon handlers he had ever met—and the precision with which bullets had met both their heads. Sweat greased his hand as he lowered the gun to the earth. He kicked it gently to Whitman. The pistol skipped and tumbled over the uneven dirt.

"Okay, here's how it's going to go." Whitman squatted to pick up the 1911, his Converse soles twisting against the ground. "We're going to my tent first to get my brother and my nephew. Then we're going to take a little walk to your favorite vehicle, meaning the one you have the key for, and we're going to take a nice little drive until we decide to drop you off. Things go well, you'll be back in time to bury your pal Henry."

A wildness flashed in Bartley's eyes.

"Yeah, sorry about him, by the way. X had to do it. Wasn't personal. Like I said before: kids, right?" Whitman tucked the 1911 in the back of his jeans beneath his dark blue button-down shirt. He motioned with his 10mm. "Now I'ma put this away, but I can bring it out just as fast. I know you believe me, because I know you're smart. Now come on." He beckoned with a hand as he turned, then turned back. "Oh, and if we bump into any of your Samaritans along the way, you better come up with a good story." He slipped the 10mm into the front left of his waistline, pulled his shirt down over it. "Let's go. You're leading the way."

Bartley started walking, stepped past Whitman, heard him follow close behind. They moved through the camp's dark aisles toward the eastern perimeter.

Bartley suffered no false hope. He knew he was walking toward death.

They detoured south, and after a few minutes, stopped in front of a blue eight-person tent. A small light from an electric lantern glowed inside.

Whitman lowered his head to the tent's zipped entrance, but kept his eyes on Bartley. "X, Mercer, we got to go. Get our stuff together and get out here." He spoke in a loud whisper.

"What?" Xavier's voice said from within the tent.

"We have to go. *Now*. No time for why."

There was no further response, just the rustling of bags, miscellaneous supplies, and personal items. Bartley recognized the sound of an ammo clip sliding out then back into a pistol.

Whitman straightened his posture.

"Bartley?" a voice said from down the aisle toward the south. Both Whitman and Bartley's heads jarred toward it.

Nora walked toward them, less than twenty yards away, a rifle hanging from her right shoulder, her face tired but friendly. She had just finished her security rounds.

Bartley could feel the dull throb of his heartbeat in his head, drubbing in his thoughts.

"Nora, hey," he said.

She smiled. "Hey, Bartley. Hey, Whitman. What are you guys up to?"

The rustling within the tent had stopped.

"We're going to make a run for Whitman and Xavier's car, bring it back here, add it to the caravan," Bartley said. "I know it's late, but with everything that happened today, we don't want someone to have a chance at it before us."

She looked at Whitman, who smiled. She looked back to Bartley. "You guys need another? I just got off my shift, but I don't mind."

Bartley flexed his chin, the corners of his mouth arcing down in feigned thought. "No, you go on and get some rest. We're going to make this trip quick and quiet. Less is stealthier."

Nora nodded. Her eyes dropped to Bartley's empty holster, flicked back up. "Okay. Well, you both be careful, okay?"

"We will. Thanks, Nora," Bartley said.

"Yeah, thanks," Whitman said.

Nora continued past them and turned right.

Whitman carefully watched her leave before looking at Bartley. "Not quite sure she bought that, but you better hope she did." He bent toward the tent. "Alright, let's go. *Let's go.*"

A murmuring sounded and was hushed within the tent. The entrance unzipped from the inside. Xavier ducked out, followed by Mercer. They both wore backpacks, and Xavier lifted a third to Whitman.

The boy appeared tearful. He didn't look at Bartley.

Whitman slung the pack on his left shoulder and motioned to Bartley. "Take us to our ride out of here."

Bartley led them north and east, cutting through the rows of tents until they reached the eastern perimeter and the small pocket of the camp where the Samaritans had allocated most of their vehicles.

Bartley's brain attempted to summon a ruse to delay what was happening, to slow down their exit—that he could say he had forgotten the car key back inside his tent—but leading two obviously highly trained killers back through the camp was not an option he was willing to risk. Even through the fog of liquor and fear, he knew he had to lead them away.

In the razored contrast of shadow and moonlight, he recognized the pearl-white hull of the Nissan Pathfinder, the SUV that had somehow become the flagship for the group's enterprise, a symbol of the Samaritans' plight, parked second in the first row of vehicles. He walked toward it, fished the remote key from his right jeans pocket, and half-turned to make a final plea.

"That's the one. There. The white Nissan," he said. "Here's the key. Take it. Go on. You don't need me."

Whitman, agitated, grabbed Bartley's arm with one hand and the car key with his other. "Yeah," he said. "I'm sure you'd politely oblige us with a head start before ringing a bell through your camp like goddamn Paul Revere." They reached the SUV. "Quit the bullshit, Bartley, and get in."

Whitman pulled his 10mm and shoved Bartley against the rear door on the driver's side, stepped around toward the front. Xavier and Mercer split silently to the passenger side.

Whitman palmed the remote key, squinted, and pressed his thumb into the unlock button. The locks thunked.

As Bartley reached for the SUV's rear door handle, everything became painted with his human experience—he knew how the handle would feel and sound when he pulled, the hollow clunk of the door opening, the slight suction of the rubber borders, upholstery stretching and parting—things so familiar in a lived life, yet alien in its foyer to death.

Blood like volcanic glass in the moonlight smacked against the side window.

Bartley wasn't sure if he saw it before or after the punch of the gunshot hit his eardrums. He looked down at himself, his body, his clothes, saw heavy spatters, then looked at Whitman, whose hand still grappled his bicep.

Whitman's head was half gone at the top, its profile a crater holding the distant moon. He fell forward against the driver's window of the SUV, blood streaking glass and hull as Bartley twisted his arm free and looked wide-eyed into the night.

"Put the gun down!" Nora shouted. She was standing along the perimeter of tents, the sights of her rifle held to her right eye. "Put it down now, Xavier!"

Bartley looked through the windows to the other side of the car.

Xavier had lifted Mercer from the ground, his arm wrapped around the boy's torso, pressing a 10mm pistol to his head. Mercer cried.

"Drop yours!" Xavier shouted back.

"You're not going to kill your son!"

"I'll do it! Drop it or I will!"

Bartley took a step backward, toward the front of the car, the end that was to Xavier's back.

"Don't you fucking think about it, Bartley," Xavier said, sideglancing at Bartley through the SUV's glass. "I see you disappear from those windows and I'll kill him." He looked back to Nora. "I'll kill him!"

"No you won't! Put the gun down! Put it down and maybe we let you walk away," Nora said.

"I'm leaving in this car, Nora! Put yours down! I'll kill him, I swear I will!" Xavier adjusted his grip on the pistol. "And he's not even my son!"

Mercer's voice heaved with confusion and terror.

The rifle dipped a few inches from Nora's eyes. Through the dark and roughly thirty yards of distance, she read what she could of Xavier's face.

"He's not my son," Xavier said again. "I killed his parents and I'll kill him too."

"Okay," Nora held her rifle up and out. "Okay. You got it. Just let the boy go." She placed the rifle on the ground.

Xavier watched her, hesitated.

"Just let him go, Xavier," Nora said.

Xavier pointed his gun at Nora. "You killed my brother!" he yelled. He aimed.

A shot tolled the night air.

Bartley flinched. The origin of the noise wasn't close to him—it didn't come from across the SUV, but from somewhere further north along the eastern perimeter.

Xavier's body flopped against the vehicle, slid down the side of it, a heavy smear of blood obstructing Bartley's sightline.

Nora picked up her rifle and walked steadily toward the Pathfinder. Tera emerged from the tents to the north, a sniper rifle held across her chest, and moved to intersect with Nora. Bartley stepped slowly around the car.

Mercer had been dropped to the ground, and now knelt crying next to Xavier's body, his small hands on the man's chest.

"Dad," he said between sobs. "Dad."

Bartley looked up as the two women approached.

"You were right," Tera said to Nora, who nodded solemnly.

And they all looked back to Mercer.

Part Two

Bartley

Bartley tucked his toothbrush into his gums, turned one of the paperback's pages held thumbed open in his left hand. His forefinger lined up the first sentence of the next page before his hand returned to the brush, the texture of paper always a sense reborn.

After another paragraph and a few more saws of the brush, he placed the book on his stool, spit, and palmed water to his mouth from a small metal basin behind his tent. He splashed a few cupped handfuls to his face, and scrubbed deeply into his eyes and beard.

"Hey, you," Marlene said from behind him, near the front of his tent.

Bartley padded his face with the hand towel that had been resting on his shoulder. He turned toward her voice.

"Marlene, hey. What's going on?"

She stepped around his tent. "Just checking in. Haven't talked to you in a few days. Not since the transmission. You okay?"

"Yeah, no. I've just had my head down, getting ready for the move. You?"

"Same."

An ARWS transmission had come over the radio four days earlier. They now had only three days left before they had to leave for a new clear zone located in southern Minnesota.

Marlene looked down. "I see you're still reading a lot." She picked the book up off the stool. "*The Stranger*, by Albert Camus. I think I've heard of him. Any good?"

A little over a month had passed since the night Whitman and Xavier were killed, the last night Bartley had had an alcoholic drink. He had replaced much of that drinking time with reading. Lewis, the camp's self-appointed librarian, had been lending him books, and helping him choose them.

"Yeah, it's good." he said.

In *The Stranger*, there was a description at the end of the book's first part, where the narrator loses control of a moment, resulting in tragedy. Bartley had read those pages four times before reading on.

Lewis had offered him other salvaged novels under Camus's name, though they were written by an Artificial Intelligence program that had been fed with all of Camus's original novels so it could mimic his style. Some of them, Lewis promised, were quite convincing, amazing even, though Bartley refused to read any book that wasn't expressed directly from another human mind.

"That's good," Marlene said. "So I heard you've been going with Joseph and Tera on their foraging expeditions. That right?"

"Yeah, just trying to help. Especially with the move coming up, we've been trying to do as much foraging as we can." Bartley had been pressuring himself to pick up Henry's share of the work, silently shouldering the blame for his absence. "I was actually going to tag along on a quick survey with Joseph this morning, but thought I'd give him a break. He's probably sick of me."

"I doubt that." Marlene smiled.

It was a smile that had the faint familiarity of the way she used to smile at him, when she had looked at him with the same eyes with which he still looked at her. Before the incident. Back when Marlene was still pregnant with Charlotte.

They had been traveling with another pair, a married couple named Nolan and Tori, whom they had helped reunite at a crumbling Long John Silver's restaurant in Minneapolis. During the final days of a clear zone in Cincinnati, the four of them had just finished loading scavenged supplies from a rear access point of a downtown city block Kroger, and after Nolan ran into the grocery store for one final item, a group of fifteen armed pirates had appeared around the street corner that Nolan's Toyota Camry had been facing. Bartley and Marlene and Tori all yelled for Nolan. Bartley was in the driver's seat, the steering wheel squeezed in his hands, the engine on. Tori panicked and opened the car door, despite Bartley shouting for her to stop. She had disappeared into the Kroger, going after Nolan. Thinking of Marlene and the unborn baby in the passenger seat, and with the pirates less than twenty yards from them, Bartley had yanked the car into reverse and accelerated away, leaving the older couple behind. Marlene screamed for him to go back. For him to turn around and go back for them. But he didn't. He knew he couldn't.

Later, Marlene told him she understood why he did what he did. That she knew he didn't have any other choice. That she was grateful. But she had never looked at him the same way again.

Bartley vacated his throat.

"So Joe tells me Ellen's doing great looking after Mercer," he said.

"Oh, Bartley, you should see her. She's like a different person."

"That's great."

"Yeah, it's got to be a relief for Joe, too."

"He definitely seems like a load's been lifted. How's the boy?"

"Still hasn't spoken yet, but he's coming along. I think his visits with Charlotte help more than anything I'm telling him. It's going to be a process, that's for sure."

"Well, you're doing your best. Kid's got a tough situation to fight through."

Marlene nodded, looked at the book in her hands, put it back down on the stool.

"Anyway," Bartley said, "I'm going to run over and check in with Amelia and make sure the fleet is running as well as it can be. Last I heard, one of the vans was giving her—"

"*Oh my god,*" Marlene said, looking past Bartley, out away from the camp to the north.

Bartley turned to see Gravedigger and eleven other men approaching from the slope that led up to the Keepers' camp. His jaw went slack as his eyes focused and he realized one of the men was Joseph, hands tied behind his back, red running from matted hair on the side of his head above his ear.

"*What the fuck?*" Bartley said.

"The hell did they do to him, Bartley?"

"Go." He spoke to Marlene without changing his gaze. "Get to Charlotte, warn the others, Marlene."

"Bartley."

"Get to your daughter."

Marlene receded from his periphery, and Bartley started toward the approaching group. His steps were slow. He met them just twenty yards from the Samaritans' camp perimeter.

Gravedigger's shovel rested on his shoulder just below the metal spade, his fingers gripping and tapping lightly on the handle, his expression stern yet unconcerned. The other Keepers with him scowled with an intense aggression, like snorting bulls kicking back dirt. Joseph seemed dazed, shaken, breathing densely, blood wetting the left shoulder of his beige shirt beneath the gash on his head—a wound Bartley assessed could have been caused by a shovel.

"The hell is this about, John?" Bartley said, his brow low and his voice biting.

"Stopping by as a courtesy, Bartley. Your man here has been found guilty of thievery and deception," Gravedigger said.

"What?"

"We caught him stealing mushrooms at our campsite. Then he lied about it."

Bartley looked at Joseph, who raised his head slightly to meet Bartley's eyes.

"I was outside their camp," Joseph said, his voice a rasp. "Just foraging."

"That was our territory and you knew it!" Gravedigger yelled. "You see, Bartley? Still lying!"

"He didn't know, John. I know Joseph. He wouldn't—"

"This isn't a discussion! Just thought I'd let you know before doling out his punishment. You're welcome." He shoved Joseph forward, southwest, with the butt of his shovel. "Move!"

The group began moving with Gravedigger and Joseph. Bartley followed alongside them.

"What punishment? What are you going to do, John?" Bartley said.

The ground was a wash of green, yellow, and orange against pale rock as their feet quickened over the volcanic plateau.

"There's only one punishment for deception."

The group was well away from the Samaritans' camp now, over forty yards and extending.

"Then it's me. I deserve the punishment. I sent him out there, John." Bartley glanced from Gravedigger to his own feet to keep from tripping. "John. John! I sent him, John. It's my fault!"

Gravedigger, still striding across the rock, turned and held up his shovel toward Bartley, the spade just a foot from Bartley's chest.

"Then I'll deal with you next!"

Bartley tried to think clearly. He looked off in the direction they walked. They were far from the camp now.

A realization broke over him, and he turned back to Joseph.

"Joe. Joe! Lie down, Joe. Stop walking. Don't cooperate with them!"

Joseph looked at Bartley. The left side of Joseph's head was swelling.

His feet slowed. Gravedigger spurred him forward with another shove.

"You make this difficult and I kill wifey next, *Joe*."

"John. *John*. Don't do this, okay? He's sorry. We're both very sorry. Okay?"

"Too late," Gravedigger said.

They approached what looked like a mound in the rocks, some kind of small hill.

"John, I'm warning you. Don't you fucking do this."

"You're warning me? Funny."

"Joe, lie down! Stop!" Bartley moved toward Joseph, but was struck hard in his clavicle by one of the Keepers with the butt of a rifle. A stinging pain almost doubled him over.

Gravedigger pushed Joseph up the mound's slope to the mouth of the geyser, the lip of what was once called "Old Faithful."

Steam rose in billows.

Gravedigger spoke ceremoniously. "Joe, you have been found guilty of your crimes, and sentenced to death by geyser."

Bartley's hand darted up and left, to the handle of his 1911 handgun. He had it halfway out of the shoulder holster when a gong of color and pain rang through his skull as the Keeper known as Light Switch hammered him in the back of the head with an old standing lamp fashioned into a staff.

Bartley dropped to his knees, blinked away the blackness swimming into his vision.

"Don't do this," he said. He looked up. "John, don't do this."

Gravedigger didn't look away from Joseph. "Any final words?"

Joseph turned around, his back to the geyser. He looked down at Bartley.

"Take care of Ellen," he said, his voice weak, resolute.

"John," Bartley said.

Gravedigger drew back his shovel sideways.

Bartley's insides boiled up into his throat.

"*Gravedigger!*" he yelled.

Gravedigger swung the shovel, hitting Jospeh in the same spot as before, and Jospeh, eyes lolling, fell backward and disappeared into the geyser's mouth, a hollow splash and slosh of superheated water fired to over 200 degrees Fahrenheit by magma chambers beneath the earth's crust.

Bartley bit down into his own teeth, lowered his head. He tasted blood. His eyes seared from squeezing shut.

He was barely aware of Gravedigger's voice. "Well, look at that. I guess I'm a chef now, too. Ay, Bartley?"

The Keepers laughed.

Bartley sank forward, his hands finding the rock, arms locking at the elbows to prop him up.

"Come on, fellas. We'll solve that fucker another time," Gravedigger said.

And the Keepers turned back north.

The Keepers

"Please," the man named Dante said. "I don't even know what you're talking about. I'm *telling you*."

Wisecracker watched as the man pled for his life from his knees, the man's right hand squeezing a bloody rag over the stump of his left pinky finger, blood running down his upturned forearm, dripping from his elbow. Gravedigger stood over him, an unlit cigar between his teeth, in his right hand a cigar cutter textured with a mix of dried and fresh blood. He worked the cutters open and closed with his thumb and middle finger, giving it the seeming of a tiny carnivorous mouth, fed and still hungry.

"And I'm telling you, I don't believe you, Dante," Gravedigger said. "So the next little piggy is going to market."

"No more. *Please*," Dante said.

"I'll even let you choose this time. Which'll it be?"

"*Please!*"

Wisecracker knew how far this could go. He also knew Gravedigger often found a way to surprise him with how far he could take it. He had once seen Gravedigger dig out a man's eye, shove it into the man's mouth, then force him to chew.

Please just admit to it, Wisecracker thought, certain of Dante's innocence. *It's going to end the same either way.*

"Whichever you choose," Gravedigger continued, "you probably won't be conscious after this next one."

"Okay!" Dante yelled.

"Okay, what?"

"I took the canned pears."

Wisecracker stared at Dante. The poor guy had wandered too far from the Washington Clan's camp, far enough away to be plucked up by Gravedigger and his patrol.

Good man, Wisecracker thought. *At least it'll be over quicker now.*

Wisecracker was convinced that there were no missing cans of pears from the Keepers' camp.

Gravedigger pocketed the cutters, pulled the shovel from resting against his back.

"And the truth shall ease your suffering."

"*Wait*," Dante said.

"Your sentence is death by shovel. Any last words?"

Dante's eyes searched the faces of the nearby Keepers, found Wisecracker's, locked onto his eyes. Wisecracker looked away.

Dante grimaced. "Yeah," he said. He looked up at Gravedigger.

Wisecracker watched again.

Gravedigger cocked the shovel above his head.

"*I didn't take any fucking pears!*" Dante yelled.

And Gravedigger swung the shovel down, turned sideways into its bladed profile, chunking into the top of Dante's head. Gravedigger ripped the shovel away and stepped around to get a better angle as Dante fell backward to the earth. Gravedigger didn't hesitate and swung again. And again.

Wisecracker was grateful that Gravedigger's body now blocked his view, but he could still hear the sounds.

He never got used to the sounds.

Gravedigger stepped back after the third swing, breathing heavily, sweat shining his reddened complexion. He turned away from the body and brought the cigar cutters back out of his pocket. He took the cigar from his teeth and cut the closed end. He tucked the cigar back into the corner of his mouth and looked around at the other Keepers.

"Light? Anybody?" he said. "No?" And he walked away from the dead body.

One of the other Keepers, Booster, immediately stepped forward, knelt and began palming the body's jacket and pants pockets, turning some of them out, with no regard for the bright red blood transferring onto his hands. He stood back up holding a small green pack of gum. He withdrew a shiny foil-wrapped stick and unwrapped it to the thin pale sugar of the plank underneath, biting into the stale flavor with a crack.

Wisecracker watched him as the other Keepers dispersed.

Booster closed his eyes as he chewed, then opened them and saw

Wisecracker watching.

Booster snapped the rest of the stick into his mouth, and stared back.

#

Gravedigger, the lit blood-hued half-smoked cigar clenched in his jaw, called out to Wisecracker as Wisecracker made his way back to his tent.

"Hey, Wise, a moment." He grabbed Wisecracker by the shoulder, turned him to walk with him in another direction. Wisecracker felt an adrenaline spike of panic. "I have a mission for you."

Wisecracker swallowed. "A mission?"

"That's right. And I'm going to need it done tonight." Gravedigger's eyes scanned the camp as he smoked, his arm extended around Wisecracker's shoulders. "Tonight, you're going to go to the Samaritan's camp, and you're going to take out their doctor, Marlene."

"Take out?"

"Kill. You're going to kill her."

"Why?"

Gravedigger took the cigar from his mouth and held it in his hand, smoke coming like a reverse waterfall from his mouth and nose. "You see, you weren't there, but last time I saw him, good old Bartley tried to pull a gun on me. You believe that? He actually tried to pull on *me*. And that's a crime that death ain't enough of a punishment for." His arm still around Wisecracker's shoulders, he leaned in closer. "I want to see him lose what he cares most about. And we all know how he feels about Marlene. You can see it every time she's around him. Plain as day."

Wisecracker was silent. Gravedigger took another puff from the cigar.

"So, you go tonight. And Done Deal is going with you."

"Why me?" Wisecracker said.

"You're asking questions now?"

"No, it's just. I was curious."

Gravedigger's arm dropped from Wisecracker's shoulders, and he turned square with him.

"You see, that question answers itself," Gravedigger said. "You're not fully committed, Wise. You think we don't see it in your face? Every time we have to lay down the law? Show some especially tough love? We all see it, Wise. Nobody likes to do the dirty work, but we all have a calling here. An obligation. We're all committed to the cause. And now you have to show us that you're committed, too." He poked a finger into Wisecracker's chest. "You get this done, we'll know for sure."

Wisecracker nodded slowly.

"And Done Deal? Well, you know why we call him what we call him, right?"

"Yeah, I know." Wisecracker said.

"Good. Go get 'em, Wise. I really don't want to have to taste your blood on the end of a cigar."

#

Done Deal moved low and quick as he followed Wisecracker through the pocket of trees on the east side of the Samaritans' camp. From the light of the full moon, he could easily see his fellow Keeper. Wisecracker had already drawn his weapons—a bowie knife in his left hand and a Colt Peacemaker revolver in his right—both hanging at his sides. Done Deal stepped next to him as they reached the edge of the trees, the land sloping down toward the camp, and they both squatted to rest on their haunches.

Done Deal could hear Wisecracker's breath, could see him trembling in his periphery.

Coward, he thought. *If that's what it's like to care, I'm glad I don't.*

Done Deal remembered what it was like to have nerves and fear, uncontrollable, pushing in on him. But then his father, just a year before the weather came, went into a gun range, rented a Glock 10mm, walked to a stall, put the gun in his mouth and pulled the trigger. Blood all over the walls.

Done Deal had been nineteen years old.

His father had taught him how not to care.

Coward.

"Her tent's about halfway between this perimeter and the center of the camp," Done Deal whispered to Wisecracker.

He looked left and saw a patrol of two men coming from the south along the camp's limits. He recognized one of the men as Caleb—young and inexperienced, someone he expected to kill at some point.

"There's a patrol," he said. "We'll wait for them to pass, then head in. I doubt they're expecting us."

Done Deal slowed his breath almost to a stop as the two men passed and headed north. Wisecracker's breath quickened.

He's going to fucking snap, Done Deal thought.

He hated Wisecracker, thought he was a silly idiot that didn't deserve the status of a Keeper. Hadn't earned his place among them. Alway looked scared, or sick, or fraught while the others did what had to be done.

Done Deal had no sympathy for him, no desire to help him prove himself tonight.

The patrol was out of sight.

"Alright. Let's go," Done Deal said.

As soon as Done Deal became aware that Wisecracker had stepped behind him, a knife entered the left side of his neck point-first, and sliced outward through the front. Trachea and vessels cut, windpipe filling with blood.

Freddie "Jammer" Jamison, known as Wisecracker by the people left in this world, watched Done Deal bleed out at the tree line, the soil around Done Deal's head a darkening mane. When all movement from the dying Keeper had ceased, Freddie picked up both of the man's arms by the hands, and dragged him deeper into the trees.

Freddie stifled a gag. His shoulders shook. He didn't want to deal with the body alone, its true burden made real with its weight in his hands. His insides screamed for help. For someone to help him. Though he would never ask.

#

As morning broke over the landscape, Freddie reached the crest of the hill to the north and walked back through its trees into the Keepers' camp.

Paladin was the first to see him and turned to an intercepting course.

"What happened?" Paladin said. "Where's Deal?"

Freddie stepped past him. Paladin walked alongside him.

"I need to talk to Gravedigger," Freddie said.

"What the fuck happened, Wisecracker?"

"I'll tell you when I tell Gravedigger."

"You'll tell me now, you son of a bitch!" Paladin stopped Freddie by the shoulder and gave it an extra shove. "Where's Deal? The fuck did you do?"

Freddie glared into Paladin's face. "Back the fuck off, Paladin. I told you, I'll tell you when I tell Gravedigger!"

"So tell him," Gravedigger's voice came from behind Freddie.

Freddie turned to face the Keepers' leader.

"Gravedigger," Wisecracker said.

"Yes, you said that already."

"It's done. Marlene's dead. I killed her myself. Cut her throat. Done Deal made sure it was me who did it." Freddie paused. His jaw released.

"We got spotted on the way out. Deal got hit. He's gone. Dead."

"That it?" Gravedigger was studying Freddie's face.

"That's it. That's my report."

Freddie had fired off two shots into the air shortly after he had hid Done Deal's body, to corroborate his story.

"You left him behind?"

"He was dead. Took one in the back of the head. That's that."

"You seem... different."

"I am. Like you said, I needed to be all in. I'm all in now."

Gravedigger stepped close to Freddie, still scrutinizing, leaning in.

Then he threw a hand up and clapped Freddie on the bicep.

"I like it!" Gravedigger said. "Welcome to being a real fucking Keeper, Wise. And just wait to you hear what we have in store for those Samaritans tonight!"

Freddie stared at him. "What do you mean?"

Gravedigger smiled.

Freddie smelled smoke and blood.

The Reaped

Michael stepped out of Tera's tent and into the early morning light.

While Marlene was dealing with Ellen's overwhelmed emotional state after losing Joseph, Tera was taking care of Mercer and Charlotte, and Michael had stopped by to check on her.

As he narrowed his eyes against the light, he quickly became aware of an unnerving commotion frothing throughout the camp, its residents. His forehead rolled back in angst.

He attuned himself to the distressed voices and frantic movement as he walked through the aisles of tents, leading him to the west perimeter where he saw a large group of Samaritans standing among the fleet of vehicles.

Bartley, Amelia, and Caleb were at the center of the group, which expanded and contracted as people walked among and around the vehicles, examining them and returning to the centralized conversation.

As Michael approached, Caleb flailed his arms.

"I'm telling you, I'm going there right now. I'm going there and I'm going to kill as many of them as I can," Caleb said. As he turned, Michael could see a large knot on the back right of his head.

"You have to calm down, Caleb. Calm down. The only way we get through this is to stay level-headed and think," Bartley said.

Michael sensed something in Bartley's voice, a quiet rage that didn't match his words.

"I'm not in Kindergarten, Bartley. Don't talk to me like I'm a kid."

"No one's talking to you like that," Amelia said.

"I don't care about dying," Caleb said. "This is..." he took a shuddering breath, "I've had enough of this shit." His hands searched his head, gripped his hair. "I can't fucking do this anymore."

"Breathe," Bartley said.

"I know how to breathe, Bartley."

"We have to have a plan."

"What's going on?" Michael said. He was at the center of the group now, twenty of their fellow Samaritans surrounding them, most of them watching. "What happened?"

"The tires, in the night," Amelia said, "they slashed all our tires." She looked at and motioned to Bartley's Nissan. "Except for the Pathfinder."

"What?" Michael said. A lightheadedness peeled through his mind. He felt suddenly hot, his pores prickling with sweat. "They got them all on each one?"

Amelia nodded.

"What happened to our patrols?" Caleb, still seething, pointed to the knot on his head. "Fuckers snuck up on us."

Michael bent over, his hands to his knees. He blinked at the ground, looked back up.

"Wait, why the Pathfinder?"

"Because he wants me to have to choose," Bartley said. "This is some fucked up kinda thing about me." He looked at Michael. "I'm sorry."

"Stop saying that. It isn't your fault, Bartley," Amelia said.

"So what do we do now, Bartley?" a Samaritan named Marsha said, standing among the gathering.

Bartley looked at her. "First, we have to stay as calm and as logical as possible. They'll expect us to act rash out of fear or anger. Or they'll expect us to give up." He looked back at Caleb, who had lowered his hands into trembling fists at his sides. "We can't do either of those things." He paused, looked to the ground, back up to the people. "The ARWS said the storm sweeps in this evening, before sundown. That's not much time. We'll put together a group to leave in the Pathfinder. To get out ahead of the storm. The rest of us... the rest of us mount an assault on the Keepers' camp. And we take the Keepers' vehicles for ourselves. All of them."

There were murmurs in the group, growls of affirmation, whispers of doubt. Nervous faces looked at one another.

"My car," Christopher said, stepping forward from the crowd. "My Honda Accord should still be where we left it, on the western rim of the clear zone. We get that, that's five more people out ahead."

"Yes, good," Bartley said. "We get as many people as we can out ahead. In the Pathfinder, it'll have to be the two kids, Marlene, Ellen," he nodded at Michael and Amelia, "Michael, Amelia, and Tera."

"Of course he picks Marlene," another Samaritan in the crowd, Sarah, said. "We all know how close they are."

"And we all know she's our doctor," Bartley said firmly. "We protect our doctor, our horticulturist, our mechanic, our kids and their mothers. And we include a strong fighter, Tera, for protection. That's it and that's that. Anybody want to argue, you have about five seconds to debate me."

The group was silent.

"Okay," Bartley continued, looking at Christopher. "We send a small group to bring back Christopher's Honda. When they get back, we have a drawing. Papers out of a hat. Anyone who doesn't want to stay and fight can enter. Five people. That's it. No trying to ride in the trunk. They're going to need room for supplies." He looked around. All eyes met his. "Alright, let's get ready then, people. We're just hours away from fighting for our lives."

As the group dispersed, Michael stepped close to Bartley.

"Thank you," Michael said. "For including Tera and me."

Bartley looked at him, then motioned to Christopher.

"Let's go get that Honda," Bartley said.

#

Bartley closed the empty ammunition box with a soft metallic clunk and placed it next to the empty long gun crate on the table within the camp's munitions tent. His eyes loitered on the crate. He shrugged at the strap of the HK416 assault rifle on his right shoulder. A satchel containing four extra 5.56mm 30-round magazines was slung on his left.

"**Last Straws**" was written in black marker on blue tape across the top of the crate. He'd hoped never to open it. The four guns he had pulled from that crate, he remembered hearing their model types or similar model types spoken too often by news anchors with sad voices after the mass shootings that occurred almost daily in the old America. Now there were no masses to shoot. He hated having one of those guns strapped to his back.

He looked around the munitions tent, walked to its entrance, processing a cigarette from his pocket to his lips. He had already divvied up and distributed weapons and ammunition to the camp members that were staying back. Not all of them carried the firepower he was carrying, but each had a firearm with which they were comfortable.

Bartley, Michael, and Christopher had returned three hours

earlier with the silver Honda Accord. The two operational vehicles were being loaded now by the group that was leaving. The rest of the Samaritans were at their tents, breaking them down and packing, readying themselves, coming to terms with the task that lie ahead.

There were just three hours before the storm arrived. The window of timing was going to be short. Shorter than most clear zone transitions.

The departing group had to leave at the front end of the designated window the route would clear, just a half hour from now, to get a head start. The remaining Samaritans had to launch their assault at that exact same time, to prevent the Keepers from leaving before the assault was underway. The Samaritans needed to capture the vehicles and be en route within just a couple hours. Maybe less.

A peephole of a time window.

By Bartley's last count, the Keepers had 22 members in their camp.

After the departure of the two vehicles, the Samaritans would have 26.

Thanks to Henry's training, all of the Samaritans knew how to shoot. Not all of them knew how to kill.

Bartley lit his cigarette, looked up at the sky. The weather was already shifting, the sun shuttered by gray clouds, an ominous stratus, matching the gloom he felt for the coming battle. The smoke slithered quicker with the breeze off the end of his cigarette.

"Bartley." A Samaritan named Karen approached from the south end of the camp.

Bartley raised his eyebrows at her in a listening fashion.

"Bartley, I can't do this. Please find a spot for me in one of the cars. *Please.*"

"I can't do that, Karen," Bartley said. "You know I can't do that."

"I'm no warrior. I'm fifty-eight. I can't fight. Please, I need to go with them."

"We had the drawing. Everybody who wanted a chance, got one. There's nothing I can do."

"Bartley..."

"Look, I'm sorry, Karen. If I had a spot, I'd give you mine. If you don't think you can fight—"

"I *know* I can't."

"Then you can stay back at camp during the assault. I'll understand. We all will. No one will judge you for it. But that's all I can tell you."

Her shoulders fell, she turned sadly away, gave a wordless half-turn back, then continued south toward her packed up tent and possessions.

Bartley's eyes followed her until he heard footfalls from the west.

"You okay, Bartley?" Marlene's voice said.

Marlene, Tera, and Michael now stood in front of him, paces away. He looked from face to face.

"Yeah," he said. "Just some people taking the results of the drawing kind of hard."

Michael stepped forward, his hands fiddling with his leather-bound horticulture journal.

"We're leaving, Bartley. We have to go." Michael's right hand left the journal, extended out toward Bartley.

Bartley took his hand tightly, shook it.

"I just wanted to thank you again, Bartley," Michael continued. "For everything." He shook his head, as if no words were enough, then nodded firmly. "Thank you."

Bartley met his eyes, nodded. "You're a good man, Michael."

Michael stepped back as Tera walked forward. She hugged Bartley.

"*Thank you*," she said, and then she cried.

"Come on now," Bartley said softly.

"I'm so sorry about Joseph, Bartley."

"It's not your fault, Tera."

"I should have been out there with him."

"Then you would be dead too."

She gave him a final squeeze, then pulled away, wiping her face as she strode back to Michael.

Marlene stood a foot from Bartley now, and it was as if everything else, the camp, the dirt, the world entire, dropped away.

Bartley had already said his goodbyes to Marlene and Charlotte earlier, after helping them pack up their belongings, and had managed to bite back his tears. Now he was both buoyed to see Marlene again and worried that his emotional steadfastness might falter.

"You know," he said. "Before all this, before the disasters, this... wicked world of weather and carnage, we had convinced ourselves, humans I mean, that our barbaric history was just that—history. Peasants beheaded on a whim; women burned because they were suspected of witchcraft; genocide. We treated this human gravity toward cruelty and violence as if it were a thing of the past. But whether by blood-soaked hands or crisp greedy white collars, it has always existed, continues to exist. We've just been joking ourselves."

"*We* haven't. Not with what we've done here, Bartley," Marlene said. She stepped close to him, her hands finding his. "*We* aren't some punchline."

Her dark green eyes danced between his.

"And besides," she said, smiling. "You've never been good with jokes anyway." Bartley smiled slant back at her.

Her smile faded and she hugged him.

"*Survive*," she said. "We'll be waiting for you. Survive, Bartley."

He felt her shoulders shaking in his embrace.

She let go and turned away.

"Marlene," he said.

She turned back toward him and her mouth went perfectly onto his, lips soft in a bending caress, opening, their tongues pressing together as if they wanted never to be separate. Their arms pulled their gravities into one another again, tighter this time. And for ten of the most eternal yet fleeting seconds of Bartley's life, he was home. There was no catastrophe, no wrong that existed.

Her mouth moved to his ear. He felt her tears warm on his cheek.

"Find us," she said, then turned away and didn't look back.

#

The evening sky churned a gray spectrum between light and darkness.

The group of 26 armed Samaritans moved low and slow up the slope to the north, toward the Keepers' camp. The landscape was quiet, colors muted. As Nora and the others crested the rise of land and neared the thicket of trees between them and their target, what sounded like an aluminum whistle shrilled among the wood, and after a moment of stillness and hesitation, a crackling burst of bullet-fire streaked among the attacking party like hornets from a kicked nest, and they all took cover behind the trees.

That had to be their watchman, Nora thought. She dropped behind a lodgepole pine, holding her M16 assault rifle vertically in front of her, parallel to herself and the tree. *They all know we're here now.*

"Get down and take cover!" Bartley yelled. He was just a few trees away from her, observing the other Samaritans, evaluating their positions and statuses.

Nora looked around too. No one seemed hit.

A 65-year-old Samaritan named Sam kneeled behind a pine directly to her right. She remembered when he had first joined their group. Like most newcomers, he had been emaciated, could barely stand for ten minutes straight. Now, he looked twenty pounds heavier. And ready to fight.

Nora was proud of what they all had accomplished as a group. As a community. As Samaritans. This was what they were fighting to save.

Like Sam, she was ready. She hadn't put her name in the hat for the drawing.

Bartley motioned. "Move! First down up!"

10 yards. Bartley had gone over the lingo with the group. All the Samaritans advanced 10 yards further into the depth of trees and repositioned themselves behind cover.

No shots fired. Only a minute had passed.

They're still scrambling, Nora thought. *It won't be for long.*

Seconds later, the patch of forest lit up with the rapid pops of gunfire, the sizzle of airborne lead, the thudding of struck earth, the cracking and splintering of living wood.

Nora pressed her back hard against the tree trunk until it hurt. A bullet hit her tree. She felt bark particles dust her face, smelled spent gunpowder.

To her left, Caleb was buckled down behind a tree of his own, eyes gaping, breathing strings of spittle through gritted teeth.

To her right, a Samaritan named Peter cried out in pain, grabbed an exposed shoulder now bloodied.

The gunfire blazed on for twenty more seconds before ceasing.

After a heartbeat, she heard Bartley yell again.

"First down up! *Let it go!*"

#

The Samaritans came from behind their trees guns up and firing.

The Keepers' return fire ignited almost immediately, like a ripsaw through the trunks. Two Samaritans fell before they could pull their triggers, shredded by the lay of bullets.

Bartley, his trigger finger unsparing, shot at what he could see of the Keepers, the flames of their barrels. He knew he had killed three before he fell behind the trunk of another pine.

He heard yells, screams. Sides indistinguishable. Like hell pouring in from all angles.

And for a moment, he forgot that he was the one who had his hands on the controls. He was the one the decisions fell to.

He heard crying, souls breaking and being reforged, the clacks of ammo clips fumbled and interchanged, a Samaritan vomiting.

Sometimes you don't realize you're dealing with your own body as much as you're dealing with the enemy.

Against a tree a few arm-lengths ahead, the Samaritan named

Daniel was praying with a shotgun in his lap, his face red and dark with soil and tears. Bartley scanned the shortening span of trees in front of him. He turned back, his hands on the rifle he hated, the controls he despised. He let go with one hand for an instant, and crossed himself. Forehead, sternum, right shoulder, left shoulder.

And then he yelled the command: "*Kickoff!*"

All Samaritans charged at once, save for a man crouched behind a fallen tree, yelling, "*Fuck, fuck, fuck!*" The air seemed electric with bullets. People fell on both sides. All around. Bartley saw Keepers between his iron sights burst into red before he could pull the trigger. He adjusted his aim, fired, and more Keepers fell. He turned his head when he heard Caleb shout, saw the young man cradling a ruptured kneecap with both hands, turning in the dirt. Bartley hit the magazine release, let the clip fall to the earth, his hand unsheathing a fresh one from his satchel, shaking with adrenaline, missing the reload twice before the clip finally clicked securely into its housing. He kept firing. He heard the Keepers shouting. Could recognize Gravedigger's voice.

Then Bartley was at the break in the trees, opening into a clearing where he could see the Keepers' vehicles to his left, mostly trucks, one motorcycle. Eight vehicles in total.

Eight vehicles. It was enough.

A bullet slammed into the tree to Bartley's left, sending a barrage of splinters into the side of his face. He dropped to a knee, fired, killed two more Keepers.

The vehicles were thirty yards away, parked closely together, mostly loaded. Bartley saw Gravedigger sprinting across the clearing toward them, a large revolver in his right hand, his shovel jostling on his back.

No you fucking don't. Bartley took off running too.

He felt the air hot with bullets around him, he reached the closest end of the clump of vehicles, ducked down between them, still moving, eyes and rifle still up. Bullets began riddling the cars, thunking metal, crashing windows. Glass shards rained across Bartley's shoulders like tiny diamonds.

Bartley tracking him, Gravedigger opened the driver's side door of a large black Toyota Tundra, threw the revolver onto the front passenger seat, unslung his shovel into the back, swung himself into the driver's seat and pushed the start button. The engine rumbled on.

Gravedigger looked through the windshield. Bartley rose a foot from the front of the truck's grill, his right eye down his rifle's sights.

"*Gravedigger!*" he yelled.

Gravedigger's hands were on the steering wheel. He dropped his right to the transmission, to pull it into drive, and Bartley fired, bullets crashing through the windshield, filling Gravedigger's face and chest, the glass turning opaque with blood.

Bartley lowered the rifle slowly, heard something land at his feet.

He looked down and saw a black grenade, pin pulled, resting near his boots.

And a brilliant flash filled his vision.

#

Bartley stood in a brightly lit kitchen at the culinary school he attended in Paris, France. The windows dim with overcast daylight and rain. The counter in front of him a smooth reflective metal. It was warm inside. He was 23 years old.

He reached forward with both hands and carefully rotated a clear glass bowl containing a deep golden brown liquid, fine-tuning its position on the spotless metal surface.

Bartley's instructor, a tall stern man with passionate eyes, graying eyebrows, and a perfectly white chef's hat, leaned over to admire the dish.

"Consommé?" the instructor asked.

Bartley nodded. "Oui, Chef." His heart beat fast—nervous, eager.

The chef took a large silver spoon and massaged it into the broth, letting it fill slowly, displaying its consistency, its color, its silk. He brought the spoon to his mouth, paused, and sipped the liquid gently.

The eyes of the other students moved between the instructor's face and Bartley's.

The instructor's eyes closed. He sipped the broth again, then placed the whole spoon into his mouth and cleaned it. He opened his eyes.

"*Parfait*," he whispered emphatically, then moved to the next student, leaving Bartley standing with an uninhibited grin, a heart heaving with joy.

Bartley saw that moment.

Then he saw Marlene and Charlotte.

Then nothing.

#

Christopher saw the grenade explode, the nearby vehicles lift from the ground, part of Bartley detach from the rest of him, then he looked away because he knew he couldn't stand to see any more.

In his new line of sight, a Keeper pulled a knife from a Samaritan's chest. Christopher raised his AK-47 assault rifle and killed him. When he turned back toward the grouping of vehicles, the Keeper named Paladin was charging at him from that direction, swinging a dripping red longsword with both hands. Christopher aimed his rifle and pulled the trigger, but it issued only a hollow click.

He looked down, his face paling, horrified, confused. The clip wasn't empty. The gun had jammed.

His entire body went hot.

Christopher looked back up. Paladin had hesitated at the aimed rifle, but now charged again, lips twisted into a bloodthirsty grin. He brought the sword back over his shoulder like reeling a fish.

And a thick spatter of blood haloed his head to the sound of a gunshot.

Paladin collapsed and slid in the dirt to a halt just two feet from Christopher's ragged tennis shoes, a grapefruit-sized section missing from the top rear of his skull, the gray tone of brain matter showing beneath.

The Keeper known as Wisecracker stood fifteen yards away, toward the vehicles, a Colt revolver raised and smoking in his right hand. He looked as stunned as Christopher felt.

Wisecracker shot Paladin.

Wisecracker turned and ran frantically toward the Keepers' fleet, to the far left end, grabbing the handlebars of the lone motorcycle and running the bike forward before twisting the right grip throttle.

"*Hey!*" Christopher yelled.

The bike rumbled and leapt forward as Wisecracker tucked his feet up onto the metal foot pegs, the engine pitching into a hum.

Christopher shook his head, turned back to his rifle, clearing it, hammering home a new clip and bringing it back up, firing in controlled bursts. Another Keeper, the one called Smoker, fell holding his neck, blood fountaining from between his fingers.

The end of Christopher's barrel oscillated over the landscape, his eye aligned down the sights. Sound died away as the scene settled. All he saw was smoke, fire, dead bodies. The air was a haze. He continued to survey the area around him, his finger on the trigger.

"Chris," a soft voice said from the tree line behind him.

He turned.

Nora stood leaning against a lodgepole pine, blood matting the hair on her forehead, her right arm holding her left shoulder, her M16 dangling from her left hand.

"Nora!" Christopher said. His rifle lowered. He stepped toward her. "You okay?"

She nodded. "Yeah. Probably not as bad as I look. You?"

"Yeah." His head pivoted to their surroundings. "We can't... We can't be the only ones left."

"I don't know." She glanced around, straightened up and walked toward him. "Looks like we might be."

Raindrops began to hit their skin. The coolness a relief. Petrichor in the air.

Thunder cascaded in the distance.

"We're running out of time," Christopher said. "Come on. Let's find a car."

They walked through the vehicles separately, starting from opposite sides and moving in.

The rhythm of the raindrops quickened, slapping against the metal and glass.

Christopher ran his fingers over the bullet holes in a Chevy Equinox's hood, looked down at the two flat front tires. He moved on to the next vehicle.

"Anything?" he said.

"No. They're all... they're all just too fucked up." Her voice was deadened by disappointment.

"These too."

They met at the final vehicle, a Jeep Cherokee.

Lightning flashed above them.

The Cherokee's windshield was gone, just a fringe of jagged glass. The tires looked okay, but the side of the SUV was honeycombed by bullet holes. Including around the gas tank.

On either side of the vehicle, they both lowered themselves down to their knees, and looked at its underside. Gasoline streamed from the bottom of the car, the growing wind pulling at the liquid.

Christopher and Nora both stood. They looked at each other over the SUV.

"There's no way for us..." Christopher said.

"No way," Nora confirmed. The wind tossed her hair.

Lightning flashed again and they both looked up at the sky, the roiling clouds like dark breathing monsters.

They both walked past the front of the Cherokee, away from the vehicles, into the middle of the clearing. They stood side by side.

The thunder swelled, grew more frequent, lightning forking to the ground less than a mile away. Rain and wind lashed their faces, small stings on their skin, their clothes soaked through and heavy.

Christopher felt Nora looking at him, and looked at her. She reach out her hand and he held it in his.

They both looked back up.

"We almost had it," Christopher said.

Nora looked at him. "What?"

"Humanity," he looked down at her. "We almost had a second chance. But we fucked it up. Like we always do."

And slowly the storm overtook them, until their hands were forced loose from one another, skin slipping from skin.

Miles in the distance, east toward Minnesota, a silver Honda Accord drove the previously allotted though still perilous path to the next clear zone, followed closely by a Nissan Pathfinder, two sleeping children in their mothers' laps, the radio dialed on.

Jacob Minasian received his MFA from Saint Mary's College of California, where he was the 2016 Academy of American Poets prize-winner. He is the author of the novella *The Places Between* (2024), the full-length poetry collection *Vestiges* (2023), and the poetry chapbook *American Lit* (2020), and his work has appeared in publications including, among others, Poets.org, Mystery Tribune, The Museum of Americana, RipRap Literary Journal, Lucky Jefferson, Windows Facing Windows Review, CP Quarterly, Red Ogre Review, multiple anthologies, and has been nominated for a Pushcart Prize. Originally from California, he currently lives with his wife and daughter in Cincinnati, Ohio.

www.ingramcontent.com/pod-product-compliance
Lightning Source LLC
Chambersburg PA
CBHW030054170426
43197CB00010B/1525